Martin McCauley is Senior Lecturer in Soviet and East European Studies, School of Slavonic and East European Studies, University of London. He has specialized in the Soviet Union for over 25 years and has published widely on the region. He has a special interest in Khrushchev and the Khrushchev period.

John Campbell is a freelance historian and political biographer. His books include *Lloyd George: The Goat in the Wilderness* (1977); *F.E. Smith, First Earl of Birkenhead* (1983); *Roy Jenkins* (1983); *Nye Bevan and the Mirage of British Socialism* (1987). He is currently writing a biography of Edward Heath. He also edited *The Experience of World War II* (1989). He is married with two children and lives in London.

Makers of the Twentieth Century

NIKITA SERGEEVICH
Khrushchev

MARTIN McCAULEY

SERIES EDITOR
JOHN CAMPBELL

CARDÍNAL

A *Cardinal* Book

First published in Great Britain in Cardinal by Sphere Books Ltd 1991

Typeset by Leaper & Gard Ltd, Bristol
Printed and bound in Great Britain by Cox & Wyman Ltd, Reading

ISBN 0 7474 0402 X

Sphere Books Ltd
A Division of
Macdonald & Co (Publishers) Ltd
Orbit House
1 New Fetter Lane
London EC4A 1AR
A member of Maxwell Macmillan Pergamon Publishing Corporation

Contents

Editor's Foreword

The last decade of the century is a good moment to look back at some of the dominating individuals who have shaped the modern world. *Makers of the Twentieth Century* is a series of short biographical reassessments, written by specialists but aimed at a wide general audience. We hope that they will be useful to sixth-formers and students seeking a brief introduction to a new subject; but also to the ordinary reader looking for the minimum she or he needs to know of the life and legacy of the century's key figures, in a form that can be absorbed in a single sitting. At the same time we hope that the interpretations, based on the latest research – even where there is not space to display it – will be of sufficient interest to command the attention of other specialists.

The series will eventually cover all the outstanding heroes and villains of the century. They can, as a kind of party game, be sorted into three – or perhaps four – types. Some can be classed primarily as national leaders, who either restored the failing destinies of old nations (de Gaulle, Adenauer, Kemal Atatürk) or created new ones out of the collapse of the European empires (Nkrumah, Jinnah). Others were national leaders first of all, but made a still greater impact on the international stage (Franklin Roosevelt, Willy Brandt, Jan Smuts). A further category were not heads of government at all, but achieved worldwide resonance as the embodiments of powerful ideas (Trotsky, Martin Luther King). The great tyrants, however, (Hitler, Stalin, Mao Zedong), are not easily contained in any category but transcend them all.

The series, too, aims to leap categories, attempting to place each subject in a double focus, both in relation to the domestic politics of his or her own country and as an actor on the world stage – whether as builder or destroyer, role model or prophet. One consequence of the communications revolution in this century has been that the charismatic leaders of quite small countries (Castro, Ho Chi Minh, Gadaffi) can command a following well beyond the frontiers of their national constituency.

At the centre of each volume stands the individual: of course biography can be a distorting mirror, exaggerating the influence of human agency on vast impersonal events; yet unquestionably there are, as Shakespeare's Brutus observed, tides in the affairs of men 'which, taken at the flood, lead on to fortune'. At critical moments the course of history can be diverted, channelled or simply ridden by individuals who by luck, ruthlessness or destiny are able to impose their personality, for good or ill, upon their times. Who can doubt that Lenin and Hitler, Mao and Gorbachev – to name but four – have decisively, at least for a time, bent the history of our epoch to their will? These, with men and women from every major country in the world, are the *Makers of the Twentieth Century*.

John Campbell
London, 1990

Chronology

1894 Nikita Sergeevich Khrushchev born in Kalinovka, Kursk guberniya, Russia.

1909 Moves to Yuzovka (now Donetsk).

1912 One of strike leaders at Bosse concern and sacked.

1914 Marries but wife dies of typhus in 1921.

1917 Becomes Bolshevik.

1918 Joins Party and fights in civil war.

1924 Marries Nina Petrovna Kukharchuk.
Leaves Workers' Faculty without a diploma.

1925 Becomes first secretary of Petrovsko-Mariinsk *raion*, Yuzovka; attends Fourteenth Party Congress in Moscow as a non-voting delegate.

1927 Attends the Fifteenth Party Congress in Moscow as a full delegate.

1928 Becomes deputy to N.N. Demchenko, head of cadres selection, Kharkov.

1929 Moves to Kiev with Demchenko and later to Moscow to enter the Industrial Academy.

1931 Elected first secretary, Bauman raikom, Moscow, then first secretary, Krasnaya Presnya raikom, Moscow.

1934 Elected member of Central Committee at Seventeenth Party Congress, then first secretary, Moscow gorkom and second secretary, Moscow obkom.

1935 Elected first secretary, Moscow gorkom.

1938 Elected to Presidium, USSR Supreme Soviet, then candidate member of the Party Politburo, then first secretary, Communist Party of the Ukraine.

1941 After German invasion becomes member of various military councils which makes him political commissar, promoted later to lieutenant-general.

1943 Re-enters burning Kiev and begins reconstruction.

1944 Elected prime minister of the Ukraine and retains his position as Party leader.

1947 Dismissed as first Party secretary of Ukraine but remains prime minister; reinstated as party leader at end of year but loses post of prime minister.

1949 Moves to capital as first secretary, Moscow obkom and also elected a secretary of the Central Committee (CC).

1953 Stalin dies; Khrushchev removed as first secretary, Moscow gorkom, but becomes head of CC Secretariat when Malenkov chooses to be prime minister; arrest of Beria opens way for straight contest between Khrushchev and Malenkov for primacy; elected first secretary, CC, CPSU.

1954 Launches Virgin Lands programme; visits China.

1955 Visits Yugoslavia; Austrian Peace Treaty signed; Geneva summit of wartime Big Four; diplomatic relations with West Germany established; travels to Burma, India and Afghanistan.

1956 Visits England; Secret Speech at Twentieth Party Congress; upheavals in Poland and revolution in Hungary; Tito visits Soviet Union.

1957 Anti-Party group defeated; Khrushchev becomes strong, national leader; *de facto* prime minister as Bulganin had sided with defeated opponents; Sputnik launched; conference of ruling Communist and Workers' Parties, and non-ruling parties; gulf between Khrushchev and Mao widens; dismisses Marshal Zhukov as minister of defence; Pasternak's *Doctor Zhivago* published abroad.

1958 Becomes prime minister; Pasternak wins Nobel Prize; conflict with Yugoslavia intensifies; relations with China deteriorate; Berlin crisis begins.

1959 Twenty-first Party Congress launches Seven-Year Plan; American exhibition at Sokolniki Park, Moscow and famous exchanges with Nixon; visits US; then China but visit not a success.

1960 Visits India, Burma, Indonesia, Afghanistan, France; Paris summit wrecked by U2 incident; attends UN Assembly and performs famous shoe banging act; Sino-Soviet split evident.

1961 First manned flight in space; meets Kennedy in Vienna; erection of Berlin Wall; Twenty-second Party Congress launches race to communism.

1962 Cuban missile crisis; confrontation with Neizvestny at Manège; bifurcation of Party and governmental apparatus.

1963 Many agricultural reforms; poor harvest.

1964 Visits Poland and falls out with Mazurov; visits Egypt and confers on Nasser and Amer title of Hero of the Soviet Union; plot against him launched; dismissed as Party and government leader and commander-in-chief of Soviet armed forces; only Mikoyan stays loyal.

1966 Begins dictating memoirs.

1971 First volume of memoirs appears; dies of heart failure.

1974 Second volume of memoirs published.

1975 Monument by Neizvestny erected.

Glossary

cadre	Communist Party functionary
Central Committee (CC)	according to the Party statutes is the leading Party body; directs activities of Party between congresses, selects and appoints leading officials, directs the work of government bodies and public organizations through Party groups within them; each republic has own CC; in reality Presidium is leading body
Cheka	secret police or Extraordinary Commission for Struggle with Counter-Revolution and Sabotage; modern name is KGB
CPSU	Communist Party of the Soviet Union; in 1917 also called Bolshevik Party
dacha	holiday home (sometimes very modest cottage or can be grand house) outside city
gorkom	Communist Party committee which runs a town or city
GRU	Main Intelligence Directorate of the Soviet military
Gulag	abbreviation for State Administration of Camps; name of prison system under Stalin

KGB	Committee of State Security or political police
Komsomol	Young Communist League
kulak	literally 'fist' but term for well-to-do peasant
krai	subdivision of republic; is an *oblast* which contains autonomous district
kraikom	Party committee which runs a *krai*
Machine Tractor Stations	Set up in early 1930s to maximize use of available machinery; disbanded 1958
MGB	Ministry of State Security or secret police; name used between 1946–53; thereafter KGB
MVD	Ministry of Internal Affairs; responsible for ordinary police (militia); merged with MGB under Beria in 1953
NKVD	People's Commissariat of Internal Affairs: responsible for police 1934–46 when commissariats were renamed ministries
nomenklatura	list of most important posts in state; and list of communists suitable for such posts
obkom	Party committee which runs an *oblast*
oblast	subdivision of republic
People's Commissar	minister before 1946
Politburo	political bureau; or key Party decision-making body
Presidium	of USSR Supreme Soviet: top policy-making body or executive committee: chairman of this body is head of state; of USSR Council of Ministers: approximates a government cabinet; of CC, CPSU: name of Politburo 1952–66
raikom	Party committee which runs *raion*
raion	subdivision of *oblast, krai* or city
Secretariat of	secretaries are responsible for the entire

the CC	Party apparat; there is a first secretary, a second secretary and so on; often also members of the Politburo
soviet	council: basic unit of local government
sovnarkhozy	Councils of the National Economy; responsible for a particular region; there were 105 in 1957, 47 in 1963 and none since 1965
USSR Supreme Soviet	highest organ of government; pretended to be parliament until 1989 when it became one; republics and autonomous republics also have Supreme Soviets
vozhd	boss

Map of the Soviet Union

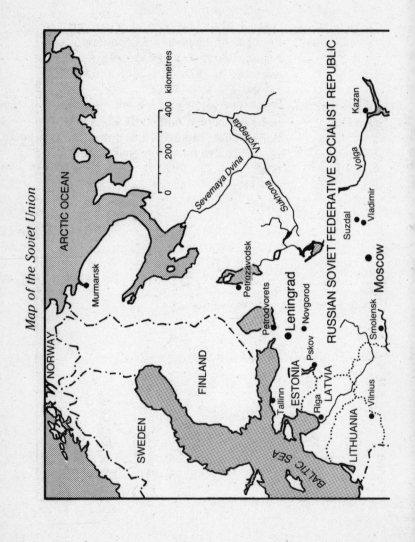

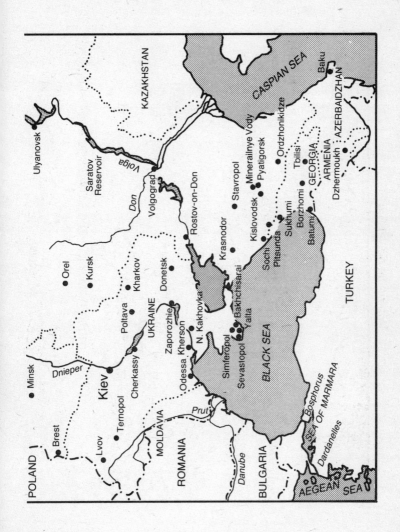

Introduction

'When Russians walk down a street they appear to be walking through a field.' This exemplifies Khrushchev's political style. He hardly ever went in a straight line and preferred to go where his inspiration took him. He was a conviction politician, believing passionately in the coming paradise of communism. This made him an optimist as regards the human potential he found in the Soviet Union – find the right administrative framework and the possibilities for material advancement would be limitless. His faith in human beings was very touching but all the more remarkable given that one of his greatest delights was to talk at length to people.

Like Gorbachev later, Khrushchev opened the window on a new era. Unlike the misanthropic Stalin he loved to tour the country and meet people. He added a human dimension to leadership. He sincerely wanted to ameliorate working and living conditions for everyone and believed that he had the tools to effect such change. However, like Gorbachev, his faith was not rewarded. The population came to ridicule his flights of fancy into the wonders awaiting them under communism. He sensed that the bureaucratic system bequeathed by Stalin was holding the country back but held to the concept of the leading role of the Communist Party. Since, in office, he rejected the market as the solution to the USSR's ills he was left dreaming about a perfect bureaucracy which would guide the country faultlessly forward. He was doomed to fail since the 'command-administrative system', as the Stalinist system is now called, cannot be made efficient.

Khrushchev's place in history is assured and he will be remembered, as will Gorbachev, as a leader who initiated a new era but who was better at describing what was wrong than prescribing solutions. He initiated reform after reform in a vain attempt to arrive at a solution to the country's ills. The very haste of reform ensured that new initiatives were ill digested before they were launched. This, in turn, ensured that their chances of implementation declined over time since officials knew that new decrees were in the pipeline. Why exert much energy when it was certain that new decrees would replace existing orders in due course?

Like Gorbachev again, Khrushchev was more popular abroad than at home. He was the delight of copy editors since he could never keep his mouth shut. He came to believe that he was an expert on everything and found criticism almost unbearable. Khrushchev was made for television but was born too early. He came out with some gems: Shakespeare was all right in his day but what was needed now were a few good proletarian writers. 'We will bury you,' after gazing at the great wealth of the United States.

Khrushchev was a paradoxical, contradictory leader. He tried to counter bureaucracy using bureaucratic methods; he denounced Stalin's personality cult and cultivated his own; he set a time limit on the occupancy of Party posts but excluded himself – he was too valuable to the nation!; he wanted disarmament and a slowing down of the arms race but told the Americans that Soviet rockets were coming off the conveyor belt like sausages and were so accurate they could hit a fly in space, thus speeding up the arms race; he wanted to do away with repression but acted dictatorially; he sought to overcome the political laws and conventions of his day but in the end was ensnared by them.

Despite his contradictions Khrushchev had a positive effect on the evolution of the Soviet Union. The '1956 generation' – those who were exposed to the denunciation of Stalin – are making their mark in the 1990s.

Early Years,

1

Nikita Sergeevich Khrushchev was a quintessential proletarian. He was born into a peasant family on 17 April 1894, in the village of Kalinovka, in Kursk guberniya. However, the smallholding was not large enough to support a growing family. As a result, Nikita's father Sergei was obliged to spend more and more time away from home seeking work during the winter. As a peasant boy Nikita Sergeevich had to make himself useful from an early age.

> Whenever I see shepherds tending their sheep now, my own childhood comes back to me. I remember looking after sheep too ... The shepherd used to send me out, saying: 'Right, Nikita, run and fetch the sheep in' – and that is just what I did ... I used to look after calves too.[1]

His rural life ended in 1909, and with it his formal education, when his father decided to become a coal miner in a pit in the Donbass region of the Ukraine. The whole family moved to a little, single-storey house outside Yuzovka (named after the Welsh entrepreneur John

4

Hughes, then renamed Stalino in 1924 and Donetsk in 1961). The town, with about 40,000 inhabitants, was expanding rapidly as an industrial centre and became a pole of attraction for peasants seeking a better life. Life was grim, dirty and hard but prospects were good. Khrushchev took any work which was going and, when fifteen, was accepted as an apprentice fitter at the Bosse factory, which was German owned. His job was to help repair mining machinery from the local pits.

Khrushchev's political education began early, in primary school. Lidiya Shchevchenko, his teacher, was an atheist who undermined his strict Orthodox upbringing. He was greatly impressed by Marx's 'Manifesto of the Communist Party' which he was able to borrow from a fellow worker in Yuzovka. Memories of the abortive revolution of 1905 were still vivid in the town and Bolsheviks became active. In 1912 Khrushchev became a strike leader at the Bosse concern but when the strike failed he was sacked. Unable to find factory work he turned to the mines and found a position as a fitter in the French-owned Rutchenkovo mine. Most politically active miners in the pit were pro-Bolshevik. Khrushchev's dynamism led to him becoming a miners' leader and a major strike broke out at Rutchenkovo in March 1915. The strikers won but this made Khrushchev a marked man. It was at this time that he became a regular reader of *Pravda*, the Bolshevik Party newspaper.

Many miners were called up in 1914 at the outbreak of war but Khrushchev was not. Increasing labour shortages led to prisoners of war, especially Austrians and Czechs, being sent down the mines. The Czechs introduced him to the heady concept of Pan-Slavism, that all Slavs are brothers and should not be fighting one another. Of all the Slavs the Czechs had the highest opinion of the Russians. This faith was to be cruelly shattered only in 1968.

The revolution of February 1917 was greeted with

unbounded joy. Khrushchev was elected to a soviet of workers' deputies at Rutchenkovo and was immediately a leading member. Although he was not yet a member, he supported the Bolsheviks. Nevertheless, when the October Revolution occurred the Yuzovka soviet was in the hands of Mensheviks and Social Revolutionaries. However, the Bolsheviks took over in December 1917 and the very active Khrushchev became chairman of the Union of Metal Workers in the mining industry. With the civil war raging he became a leader of the Rutchenkovo miners' batallion and also a member of the Bolshevik Party. Early 1918 saw the military situation worsen as German troops invaded, smashing Red Army resistance. Khrushchev escaped and headed back to Kursk. He was quickly posted to a Red Army division as a political agitator and propagandist, duties for which he was ideally suited. As political commissar he played an active part in the bloody civil war in the south. It was a formative experience for him and he always retained a special affection for military men. There is an army adage about there being two types of men: those who have been under fire and those who have not. Khrushchev was often under fire and escaped death many times. He was brave and resourceful and led by example. He carried these virtues over into his political life.

The Yuzovka and the Donbass which Khrushchev returned to had been ruined by the civil war. To this wider tragedy was added a personal tragedy. His wife, Yefrosinya (they had married in 1914), died of typhus in the dreadful year of 1921, leaving him to bring up two children, a son and a daughter, on his own.

The harsh realities of the situation demanded harsh solutions. The Donbass was the key source of energy for the fledgling Soviet republic. Mobilized workers and volunteers were rushed to the region after liberation and life and discipline were hard, with hunger a constant companion. Khrushchev became political leader of the

Rutchenkovo area and was responsible for sixteen pits.

Lenin launched the New Economic Policy at the Tenth Party Congress in March 1921. It was forced on the Bolsheviks since the country was facing collapse. It restored private enterprise and a mixed economy. The peasants, who made up 80 per cent of the population, welcomed it but communists and many workers opposed it. They regarded it as a betrayal of the revolution. Nevertheless it was an astute political move by Lenin and led to rapid recovery of the economy. Things in the Donbass got worse rather than better in 1921 due to the severe drought. As miners fled to find food elsewhere, coal output dropped sharply. The food situation improved in early 1922 and payment in kind was introduced. The more coal a miner cut the more bread he got. This boosted output dramatically.

Khrushchev's experience in the mines made his lack of technical qualifications painfully clear to him. If one was to get on one had to acquire a diploma. Fired with academic ambition he managed to get the Party to send him to the Yuzovka Workers' Faculty when it was established. But he was not merely going as a student. He was elected Party secretary and political leader of the institution. His future was taking shape. He was not destined to produce things; he was to organize people so that they could produce more. His family life also acquired more direction. He married Nina Petrovna Kukharchuk, a lecturer at the Workers' Faculty. They were to have three children, a son, Sergei, and two daughters, Rada and Elena.

The first engineers graduated from the Faculty in 1924 but although Khrushchev was a member of the award-making body he did not receive a diploma. His talent for Party work took precedence and in 1925 he was made first secretary of Petrovsko-Mariinsk *raion*. Khrushchev was starting near the bottom. It was only the sixth largest *raion*, as regards Party membership, in Yuzovka. As such he qualified as a delegate – albeit with a consultative vote – to the Fourteenth Party Congress in Moscow in 1925. It was a great occasion for Nikita Sergeevich. Housing was rudimentary. Everyone slept on planks, stacked together like logs. The secretary of the Kharkov organization slept with his wife in a row with the rest of the comrades. This led to some amusing remarks. So new was Khrushchev to Moscow that on the first day he took a tram to the Kremlin but ended up somewhere else. After that he decided to walk, setting out early to be sure of getting to the Kremlin in good time. So keen was he to get a good seat and be near the Party leadership that he skipped breakfast on one occasion. The Ukrainian delegation was headed by Lazar Kaganovich. The paths of Kaganovich and Khrushchev were to cross and criss-cross over the next thirty years.

The Congress saw a violent struggle between Stalin and Zinoviev, head of the Leningrad delegation. Nikita Sergeevich contented himself with supporting the 'General Line', which meant, in effect, backing Stalin. Moiseenko, head of the Yuzovka delegation, was much more decisive. He distinguished himself by helping to shout down Stalin's opponents. One presumes that Nikita Sergeevich howled as loudly as his leader. The Party general secretary made quite an impact on Khrushchev. The master of simulated modesty, fair-mindedness and approachability cultivated the provincial delegations. On one occasion a group photograph of the delegation with Stalin was being organized. The photographer gave precise orders. Stalin interrupted him: 'Comrade Petrov loves to order people around. But that is now forbidden here. No one may ever again order anyone else around.'

Khrushchev was a successful Party secretary and by the beginning of 1927 coal output in the Donbass exceeded the pre-1914 level. He became a full delegate at the Fifteenth Party Congress at the end of 1927. The running battle between Stalin, Rykov and Bukharin – the

Right – and Zinoviev, Kamenev and Trotsky – the Left – was to reach a climax at the congress. The Ukrainian delegation was firmly on Stalin's side. The delegation was informed – behind closed doors and with all non-Ukrainian communists excluded – about the latest state of the conflict and tactics were agreed. It liaised closely with the Moscow delegation.

Rykov, in supporting Stalin, hit on a gimmick. He mounted the platform flourishing a broom. 'I hereby hand this broom to comrade Stalin to sweep away all our enemies,' he proclaimed. He was not to know that the same broom would sweep him away a decade later. The congress took his advice. Zinoviev and his supporters were defeated and many expelled from the Party.

However, all was not well with the Stalino Party organization. During the winter of 1927–28 the Ukrainian Party initiated an investigation and the subsequent report damned the Stalino leadership for encouraging widespread corruption, drunkenness and other misdemeanours. There was a large-scale purge with Moiseenko going to a minor region. Khrushchev skilfully emerged as one of the winners.

A stroke of luck came his way in early 1928. The Ukrainian Party leadership, then in Kharkov, was on the lookout for good 'proletarian elements' since it was felt that too many officials had intelligentsia origins. Nikita Sergeevich was offered the post of deputy to N.N. Demchenko, head of the organization department which was responsible for selecting cadres. He was in two minds about taking the job since it meant moving to Kharkov where he had no contacts. He did not take easily to organizational work.

It was nothing but paperwork. I'm a man of the earth, a man of action, a miner. I'm used to working with metals and chemicals. I have a constitutional block against clerical work – it's completely alien to me. I hate having to go through a pile of forms and files to see the flesh and blood world.[2]

He kept asking for a move and the next year he went to Kiev with Demchenko who headed the organization department. He had never been to Kiev before and on arrival rushed to the banks of the Dnieper, suitcase still in hand, to gaze at the famous river. Kiev was a difficult posting as it was a centre of Ukrainian nationalism and there were considerable economic difficulties. Khrushchev deployed his interpersonal skills to good effect and became quite effective. As his horizons widened he grew in self-confidence. His ambitions began to grow as well. If an official's career was to take off he had to make for Moscow, capital of the communist universe. When Nikita Sergeevich heard about the Industrial Academy in the capital, he saw it as a golden opportunity to climb the promotional ladder. The main remit of the Academy was to train cadres for leading positions in the industrial administration. With the launching of the first Five-Year Plan in 1928 there would be bright prospects for communists with technical qualifications. Khrushchev's terrier-like persistence convinced the Ukrainian Party leadership that he would be of more value to the Party with additional technical expertise. At thirty-five it was his last chance to sit in a lecture hall as a student. The main reason why he was chosen to attend such a prestigious academy, however, may have been Stalin's desire to take over the institution. The Academy, in the main, supported Bukharin and the Right in the conflict over industrialization and collectivization. Stalin favoured a headlong rush to industrialize and collectivize, arguing that there were no limits to what could be done. Bukharin favoured the organic growth of the whole economy, with agriculture playing an important part. Stalin's proposed growth rates seemed absurdly high to the Bukharinites.

Stepping Stones to Power,

2

Immediately on entering the Academy Khrushchev threw himself into the fight against the 'Right deviationists' who then dominated the Party organization. He was convinced that Stalin's 'General Line' was correct and had unquestioningly accepted the sentences passed on the engineers from Shakhty, in the Donbass, who had been accused of 'wrecking' on behalf of the previous mine owners in 1928. He was too naïve to see that the whole affair, even though it had involved men from his own area, had been fabricated as part of a campaign to intimidate the intelligentsia. Few technical specialists sided with Stalin against Bukharin.

Not surprisingly the Academy tried to give Khrushchev the push, pointing out to him that its goal was to train senior management. He was just not qualified to be a student there. It was suggested that he was better qualified to study Marxism-Leninism at the Central Committee's institute. He would probably have been turfed out had it not been for the backing he received from Lazar Kaganovich. Khrushchev knew him well since he had previously been Party leader in the Ukraine. He was now a secretary of the Central Committee and a very tough

Stalinist indeed. Also, Khrushchev was a privileged student. He had a room of his own. This was extremely rare and appears to confirm the view that his primary task was to make the Academy a Stalinist bastion.

Party conflict at the Academy reached a peak when the delegation elected to represent the Academy at a Party conference of the Bauman *raion*, in Moscow in 1930, turned out to be anti-Stalinist. Khrushchev did not participate in the election since, in order to get him out of the way, he had been sent off to inspect an Academy collective farm. When he got back he was called to *Pravda*'s offices and signed a letter attacking the way the delegation had been elected. The delegation was recalled and Khrushchev became a member of the new one. He soon became secretary of the Party organization. He wasted no time in transforming the Academy into a battleground for Stalin's 'General Line' and resolutions passed at Party meetings often appeared in *Pravda* the next day. So the name of Khrushchev gradually became known to the Moscow Party organization and beyond that to members of the Central Committee. He enthusiastically supported rapid industrialization and forced collectivization; the conviction of the Industrial Party, accused of being in the pay of the French; and the sentencing of 'bourgeois specialists' who were found guilty of opposing the industrialization drive. He did not actually spill any blood but he did have blood on his hands.

A fellow student at the Academy was Nadezhda Alliluyeva (mother of Svetlana Alliluyeva), Stalin's wife. Astonishingly few students realized that the modest woman who travelled to classes by tram was the wife of the country's leader. Nikita Sergeevich and she hit it off and she undoubtedly mentioned him to Iosif Vissarionovich. Khrushchev was too minor to have Stalin as a patron; that role was performed by Lazar Kaganovich. The latter had become Moscow city and *oblast* (gorkom and obkom) Party leader. Khrushchev's Academy performance won him nomination as first Party secretary of Bauman *raion* (raikom) in 1931. So his academic career ended after just fourteen months, without any formal qualifications. It is fair to assume that his studies there were not theoretical – he later claimed that his life was so busy that he had no time to read books – but practical. He therefore graduated with first-class honours in Stalinism.

He stayed only six months in Bauman *raion* and was then made first secretary of the famous Krasnaya Presnya *raion*. He replaced M.N. Ryutin who had penned a vitriolic attack on Stalin and Stalinism – known as the Ryutin Platform. Stalin remained and Ryutin was exiled to the back of beyond. Khrushchev again acted as fireman and extinguished all vestiges of 'Ryutinism' in the *raion*. In January 1932 he was elected second secretary of the Moscow gorkom. He became a member of the Central Committee at the Seventeenth Party Congress in 1934 and as such a member of the Party elite.

Shortly afterwards he became first secretary of the Moscow gorkom and second secretary of the Moscow obkom. This elevated him to the position of Kaganovich's deputy but again he did not stay long in office. Soviet transport was in a critical state and badly needed a dynamic administrator to reorganize it. Lazar Kaganovich was best qualified for the post and he duly became commissar of transport. Up stepped Khrushchev to take over from Kaganovich as Moscow obkom first secretary. He was now the master of Moscow city and the surrounding *oblast*.

Why was his rise so meteoric? Was it because he was the right man in the right place at the right time? There is undoubtedly some truth in this. Khrushchev has referred to his lucky lottery ticket. Had the Academy been a Stalinist stronghold he would not have been afforded the opportunity to make his mark. Had Kaganovich's career not prospered neither would his. Had Stalin lost the factional battle Nikita Sergeevich would have found himself working again in a pit as a fitter. He learnt early to be a hundred per cent politician, either a hundred per cent for or a hundred per cent against. Never be wishy-washy.

> I was a hundred per cent faithful to Stalin as our leader and our guide. I believed that everything that Stalin said in the name of the Party was inspired by genius, and that I had only to apply it to my life.[1]

His rapid rise was not due merely to his obsequiousness towards Stalin. He was capable of delivering the goods. The Moscow press referred to his great dynamism and persistence, his 'Bolshevik toughness' (a euphemism for ruthlessness towards friend and foe alike) and his ability to instil discipline and inspire sacrifice from subordinates and the Moscow population at large.

After becoming Party leader in Bauman *raion* Khrushchev began to visit Stalin's home regularly. Stalin never invited wives or girlfriends. He appears to have had an 'oriental' attitude towards women. They were not to meddle in politics. Nadezhda Alliluyeva's death in November 1932 was a terrible shock. She took her own life after discovering that Stalin had been sleeping with another woman. After the celebrations marking the October Revolution Stalin had gone, with others, to Kliment Voroshilov's flat to drink and dine. Stalin then went on to a dacha with an officer's beautiful wife. Nadezhda, very concerned about his lateness, phoned around and was told everything. When Stalin arrived home in the morning Nadezhda was dead. Stalin mourned her loss but his guilt was mixed with feelings that she had let him down. The true story of her death only came out after Stalin's death in 1953. He never remarried and was not seen in public consorting with women. However, Lavrenty Beria procured luscious ladies for him in private. Khrushchev remembers catching a glimpse once of a black-eyed Caucasian beauty who on encountering him scurried away 'like a mouse'.

Stalin vented his spleen on some women. He delighted in being crude and rude towards Lenin's widow and sister, both of whom had sided with Bukharin. He told Krupskaya that the Party was thinking of appointing someone else as Lenin's widow! Khrushchev stated later that he was pained by Stalin's behaviour but regarded it as all part of the 'General Line'. Nikita Sergeevich learnt early not to broach a subject until it was raised by the boss. Stalin never invited criticism of his policies or decisions. Life was strictly hierarchical. When Khrushchev became Party leader in Moscow he was described as Com. Khrushchev in a Moscow newspaper. He was 'an outstanding representative of the post-October generation of Party workers, educated by Stalin'. It went on:

> Under the guidance of that notable master of the Stalin method of working, Comrade Kaganovich, N.S. Khrushchev has grown step by step with our Party in recent years and is a worthy leader of our glorious Moscow Party organization.[2]

This first mention of Khrushchev rates him Com., not Comrade. That accolade is reserved for Kaganovich. The highest plaudits of all are for Stalin; initials and the word Comrade are superfluous in his case. The hierarchy is very clearly spelled out. Khrushchev is not yet in Kaganovich's league and the latter will never be in Stalin's league.

Khrushchev now occupied one of the key Party posts but his power was circumscribed due to the fact that Moscow was the capital and the seat of Stalin. The *vozhd* or boss took a keen interest in architecture and engineering. He was also exercised by natural functions. After a May Day parade attended by many foreign visitors Stalin ordered Khrushchev post-haste to build forty urinals in the city. The foreign guests had, apparently, been put to some considerable inconvenience by the lack of loos. Moscow was becoming a European city.

Moscow was a huge building site during the 1930s. The old capital was gradually replaced by huge, modern buildings. Palaces of Culture, ministries, office blocks, parks and blocks of flats sprang up. The Stalinist style of architecture gradually developed. The *vozhd* would take a huge, ugly edifice and proceed to adorn it like a caterer decorating a wedding cake. The result was certainly no improvement on what had been demolished. In a city blessed with almost limitless space, tall buildings shot up everywhere. The thinking seems to have been that since America had skyscrapers so too must Moscow. What was overlooked was that America had lifts that worked whereas they were either non-existent or didn't function in Moscow. The capital was also becoming a great industrial base. However, pride of place must go to the Moscow metro, a marvel of modern engineering. It was begun in 1931 and the first line was opened in the mid-1930s. It was a stunning achievement and Khrushchev was a dynamo of activity, working at times alongside the crews in order to help solve technical problems. The metro was to serve three functions: a transport network; an underground palace which would be a foretaste of the communist tomorrow; and an air raid shelter, were Moscow to be bombed. It also provided a great psychological boost to the building of socialism. It was the finest underground system in the world. But a fearful price had to be paid to construct it. Safety precautions were ignored in the race to complete it. As a result thousands of workers were killed or injured. It was typical of Stalin's attitude. When someone pointed out the loss of life in building the Moscow–White Sea canal, Stalin replied that it didn't matter. The canal would last for ever.

This callousness was evident during the purges. A

conscious effort was made to degrade humans and they were referred to as vermin, mad dogs, rats and the like. This made it almost normal to kill them. It had long been a Bolshevik tradition, ably practised by Lenin, to exaggerate the faults of political opponents and accuse them of imaginary misdemeanours. Stalin took it one step further and accused his opponents of wishing to wreck the Soviet Union, sell out to fascism and murder him and the leadership. Stalin's political opponents had been defeated by the mid-1930s but the *vozhd* lived in fear of their making a comeback, were the great experiment to falter.

Stalin came low down in the voting for the Politburo at the Seventeenth Party Congress in 1934. Some of those opposed to Stalin as Party leader asked Sergei Kirov, the popular Leningrad leader, to stand. He turned this down and, moreover, reported the matter to Stalin. Kirov was murdered on 1 December 1934 by a certain Nikolaev. The People's Commissariat for Internal Affairs (NKVD), firmly in Stalin's grip, swung into action, aided by draconian new decrees. Five hundred Leningraders confessed to the crime and a quarter of the population was arrested. Khrushchev was caught up in the collective hysteria of plot and counter-plot. The old nobility and middle classes were turfed out of Moscow, as socially undesirable elements, beginning in 1935, and as a key official he gave his assent. This was mild compared to what was to come later. The greatest excesses were evident in 1937 and 1938 when millions were jailed and shot, including thousands of Party officials. (A recent estimate of the number of Stalin's victims is twenty million.) Khrushchev knew some of them personally. His language was nevertheless as vituperative as that of Kaganovich or Molotov. 'These despicable traitors infested the Party apparatus, and some of them were actually members ... of the Moscow Party Committee.'

One of his tasks was to do the rounds of the jails in

Moscow, accompanied by the NKVD. He met many former colleagues there. One Treivas was an 'intelligent, capable, decent man' but he didn't 'escape the mincer when the butchery began in 1937'. On the whole accusations, often based on denunciations, had to have some basis in fact before 1937. After that anything would do to fulfil the plan. Some of the accusations were patently absurd. Kaganovich's brother, the minister of aviation, was accused of being in the pay of the Germans. It was claimed that they were going to install him as ruler of Moscow. The Nazis would choose a Jew as the Gauleiter of Moscow! He should be so lucky!

The Show Trials were the greatest show in town in the late 1930s. The first generation of Bolshevik leaders was wiped out, all competing with one another to abase themselves. They confessed that they were the sworn enemies of Soviet power, in particular of Comrade Stalin. Naturally they had all plotted to kill him. If there is a rational explanation for the blood letting it was to cow the Party, all institutions of state and the population in order to make Stalin's position unassailable.

Why did Khrushchev, one of the top dozen in the Party, do nothing to stem the tide of mayhem? Was it due to moral myopia or moral cowardice? Or is it possible that he believed that it was all for the good?

Part of the answer lies in the relationship between Khrushchev and Stalin. It was a master–servant relationship. Stalin seems to have mesmerized the uneducated, unsophisticated Moscow Party leader.

> I was literally spellbound by Stalin … Everything that I
> saw and heard when I was with him bewitched me. I
> was absolutely bowled over by his charm.[3]

This does not, of course, excuse Khrushchev from complicity in Stalin's crimes. He was politically and morally responsible to the nation and only came to realize much later that he had failed in his duties. Khrushchev must have possessed considerable skills in order to win Stalin's confidence. The latter was a notoriously suspicious, even paranoid personality. Khrushchev himself was once fingered by Nikolai Ezhov, head of the secret police.

> I was standing around and Stalin came over and asked, 'What's your name?' 'Comrade Stalin,' I said in surprise, 'I'm Khrushchev.' 'No you're not,' said Stalin brusquely. 'Someone tells me that you're really called so-and-so. I can't remember the Polish name he mentioned, but it was completely new to me.' 'How can you say that, Comrade Stalin?' I replied. 'My mother is still alive. You can ask her. You can check at the plant where I worked, or in my village of Kalinovka in Kursk.' 'Well,' he answered. 'I'm just telling you what I heard from Ezhov.'[4]

This occurred at a time when Polish communists living in the Soviet Union were being liquidated as class enemies. There is a Russian proverb which states that the nearer one is to the prince the nearer one is to death. This did not apply to Stalin's inner circle. While thousands of fervent Stalinists perished without having opposed the *vozhd*, this never occurred to anyone in Stalin's entourage unless he had actually plotted against the master.

In order to carry out his duties effectively and to obtain intelligence about the way the political wind was blowing Khrushchev had to develop the skills of coalition building. Coalitions are like concentric circles. The inside one is the tightest, with succeeding ones becoming looser. The inner coalition included Nikolai Bulganin, chairman (mayor) of the Moscow Executive Committee between 1931 and 1937 and then prime minister of the Russian Federation, whose capital was Moscow. Another important acquaintance was Georgy Malenkov, an official of the Moscow obkom between 1930 and 1934 and then deputy head of the Leading Party Organs of the Central Committee. They all had something else in common. Their patron was Kaganovich. The looser coalitions must have been wrecked several times during the purges but every axed official had to be replaced. Khrushchev, in turn, could try to play patron. As the Russians say, the greater the patronage the longer the 'tail'.

The 1936 Soviet Constitution was the most democratic in the world, according to Stalin. There is considerable justification for this statement, providing one is referring only to the concepts which found expression there. They were never put into practice under the *vozhd*. The modern shape of the USSR dates from this time. One of its provisions was for a USSR Supreme Soviet. It only became a parliament under Gorbachev. At the first meeting of the Supreme Soviet in January 1938 Khrushchev was elected to its presidium, underlining the fusion of Party and state functions under Stalin. A plenary session of the Central Committee ran concurrently and at this more important meeting Nikita Sergeevich was elected a candidate member of the Politburo. This meant formally that he could attend Politburo meetings, speak but not vote. This was academic, however, because Stalin was not in the habit of calling for a vote in the Politburo. This was his formal election but he appears to have been attending Politburo meetings since 1935.

His formal promotion was accompanied by a new assignment. He was made acting Party leader in the Ukraine in January 1938 and his writ was simple. Make the republic safe for Stalin. There had been considerable resistance to collectivization and the republic had suffered the terrible famine of 1932–33. The purges hit the Ukraine very hard and devastated official bodies. For instance, the Party leadership had been eliminated by the end of 1937. In June Khrushchev was confirmed in office and was also elected first secretary of Kiev obkom. Only three of the previous year's eighty-six members of the Central Committee had survived. Khrushchev was fashioning a new Party apparatus and a new government – his Party and his government. He made it abundantly clear what his priorities were. 'I pledge to spare no effort in seizing and annihilating all agents of fascism, Trotsky-ites, Bukharinites, and all despicable bourgeois national-ists in the Ukraine.' Obviously he was very successful since the Party newspaper reported that the 'merciless uprooting of the enemies of the people – the Trotskyites, Bukharinites, bourgeois nationalists, and all other spying fish – began only after the Central Committee of the All-Union Communist Party sent the unswerving Bolshevik and Stalinist, Nikita Sergeevich Khrushchev, to lead the Central Committee of the Ukrainian Communist Party.' Stirring stuff but ludicrously false reporting.

Since the Ukraine was the bread basket of the country Khrushchev had to add another string to his bow, that of agriculture. Natural conditions, including the fertile *chern-ozem* or black earth, favoured crop and animal hus-bandry but the southern part of the republic was often subject to drought. If socialist agriculture could not succeed in the Ukraine, it could not succeed anywhere.

The year 1939 brought war. The Stalin–Hitler Pact led to the Soviet invasion of Poland and the acquisition of the Western Ukraine, almost all of which had been part of the Russian Empire. Khrushchev saw active service but only as a political commander. After annexation the region had to be purged and many Jews, Poles and Ukrainians were packed off to the Soviet east. Industry and trade were nationalized and agriculture collectivized. In June 1940 Romania was forced to give up Bessarabia and the northern Bukovina. The Ukrainian-inhabited parts were added to the Ukraine and the rest became the Moldavian Soviet Socialist Republic. At the same time the Baltic states were annexed by the Soviet Union.

Khrushchev displayed greater perspicacity about the

possibility of war than his mentor, Stalin. The Soviet leader persisted in the belief that his pact with Hitler would keep the USSR out of the Second World War. He trusted the Führer to keep his side of the bargain. Why he did so is still an unsolved mystery. He ignored all warnings of the Wehrmacht's plans for imminent attack. Khrushchev was alarmed by the complacency which he found on the Ukrainian front. Some tank units had no ammunition and they were in the front line! His pleas to Stalin went unheeded.

The German invasion on 22 June 1941 transformed Khrushchev into a political-military commander. His membership of the Military Council of Kiev Special Military District made him political commissar of the district. As such he was the district commander's deputy for political affairs. All military units had their own political departments and they in turn were subordinate to Khrushchev. These were not new duties for Nikita Sergeevich. Top Party leaders automatically become members of the local military council. Party control of the military is exercised through the main political administration of the military. Khrushchev, in peacetime, would have had a high military rank. His role was potentially very significant since he had the right to participate in all key military decisions in the Ukraine. When war broke out the military became his principal concern. The Party, government, industry and agriculture remained his responsibility but their focus changed. Their prime objective was to organize for victory and to provide the military with all the resources it needed. The military received its orders from the General Staff and it in turn from Stalin as commander-in-chief. Khrushchev became a vital link in the military chain since he had access to the *vozhd* both as political commissar and Party boss of the Ukraine.

War restored sanity to the Russian language. Talk of Rightists, Centrists, Leftists, Trotskyites, Zinovievites,

Bukharinites, Right Deviationists, Left Deviationists, bourgeois nationalists, enemies of the people and wreckers had all become very confusing and had debased the language. Could one and the same person be a Trotskyite, a Leftist, a Left Deviationist, an enemy of the people and a wrecker? The politically astute made sure they did not answer this question. After all they might be accused of a deviation! This extraordinary misuse of language may have been largely due to the modest intellectual credentials of the second wave of the Bolshevik leadership. Among Stalin's entourage, probably only Molotov was capable of speaking and writing correct grammatical Russian. The population at large was even more mystified.

It became necessary in the desperate days after the invasion to speak the unvarnished truth and to convey orders in crisp, understandable language. Stalin also changed tack. When he addressed the nation on 3 July he startled many by referring to them as brothers and sisters. He called for a crusade not to save communism but the nation.

An urgent task was to save as much industrial capacity, transport, equipment and so on as possible from the advancing Wehrmacht. This mammoth task required the dismantling of whole factories and their reassembly far behind enemy lines in the Urals, West Siberia, Kazakhstan and elsewhere. About a third of industrial capacity was shipped eastwards and reassembled. Khrushchev played his part in this extraordinary episode. The slowing down of the German thrust was of great importance since it afforded time to move resources eastwards. Feverish efforts were undertaken to relaunch production and overall considerable success was achieved.

It took Stalin about two years to learn the ground rules of modern mechanized warfare. He had almost decapitated the Red Army during the purges and remained deeply suspicious of the High Command during the early stages of the war. Gradually he showed more trust and faith in the top military but the armed forces paid dearly for Stalin's incompetence. Khrushchev did his best on the Ukrainian front but lost several battles with Stalin. For example, the military and he wanted to abandon Kiev to the advancing Germans then regroup elsewhere but Stalin overruled them. This meant heavy losses. On another occasion Khrushchev favoured calling off the Kharkov offensive in March 1942 after German forces threatened to cut off advancing Red Army troops. He telephoned Stalin twice but could only speak to Malenkov. Stalin, according to Khrushchev, refused to come to the phone. The advance continued, resulting in a severe defeat for the Red Army, including 150,000 troops being taken prisoner. Khrushchev was summoned to Moscow and feared the worst. However, all that happened was that he was made a member of the Stalingrad Military Council and despatched to organize defences. His main task was to boost morale and he displayed considerable bravery when moving about the front. After the epic victory at Stalingrad, in early 1943, a key turning point in the war, Khrushchev was sent to the Southern Front and partici-pated in several successful offensives and the liberation of parts of the Ukraine. Lieutenant-General Khrushchev received his first military decoration, the Order of Suvorov, second class, for 'skilful and courageous execu-tion of military operations'. Victory at Kursk allowed the Red Army to go on to the offensive for the rest of the war. It opened up the way to the Ukraine and Kiev was liberated on 5–6 November 1943. Khrushchev entered the burning, shattered city with the troops and immediately began the task of reconstruction. The Red Army carried on its advance but Nikita Sergeevich's war was over. In 1944 he was appointed chairman of the Council of People's Commissars of the Ukraine or, more simply, prime minister. He retained his position as first secretary of the Communist Party of the Ukraine. He was answerable to no one in the Ukraine but his master in Moscow.

The Ukraine which Khrushchev returned to was in an appalling state. A theatre of operations for over three years, it saw the retreating Germans and their allies attempt to destroy everything of value. Moscow rule had never been popular in the republic and the greatest opposition to collectivization had occurred there. Many Ukrainians welcomed the Wehrmacht as liberators but German policy was crude and coercive and failed to capitalize on the undercurrent of hostility to Stalin. Then there was the Western Ukraine, annexed from Poland in 1939. A Ukrainian Insurgent Army formed there and was to keep up an armed struggle against Moscow rule until the early 1950s. The region was also the stronghold of the Ukrainian Catholic Church which vigorously opposed fusion with the Russian Orthodox Church. The usual Stalinist way of dealing with nationalist opposition, deportation to Siberia, affected hundreds of thousands from the Western Ukraine.

The war changed Khrushchev. He came to see that the excesses of the 1930s had been misguided. The trials and tribulations of the common military struggle gradually brought home to him that, if inspiringly led, human beings were capable of performing great deeds. This was to get him into trouble with Stalin. Being so successful in the Ukraine had also won him enemies in the master's entourage in Moscow. Character assassination was a highly developed art under Stalin.

Restoring the Ukraine to its pre-war condition required Herculean efforts and Khrushchev led by example. The desperate need to expand agricultural output led to close contact with the rural sector. One of the crops he encouraged farmers to grow was maize. Parts of the republic are suitable and maize is a valuable fodder crop. In the 1950s Khrushchev was to develop a 'craze for maize' and be disparagingly referred to as a maize freak because of his desire to see the crop growing everywhere in the

Soviet Union. The weather did not help him. Drought in 1946 led to a halving of the grain crop and widespread hunger. When he appealed to Stalin for help he was contemptuously waved away. Stalin always bore a certain animus towards the Ukraine. It was nationalist, had resisted collectivization and had, from his point of view, a blemished war record. In his memoirs Nikita Sergeevich speaks of rumours put about by his critics in Moscow that he was becoming a Ukrainian nationalist himself.

Worse was to follow. The most serious setback to his political career occurred in March 1947 when he was sacked from three of his posts: first secretary of the Ukrainian Party, and of Kiev city and *oblast* committees. However, he remained Ukrainian prime minister. The comrade who replaced him was Lazar Kaganovich. Along with Kaganovich came Nikolai Patolichev to take over the agricultural portfolio. No overt accusations were made against Khrushchev, just the bald announcement that he had been deprived of his Party functions. To the cognoscenti it looked as if Khrushchev was being prepared as the sacrificial lamb for the republic's failures. He disappeared from view during the summer, partly due to serious illness. Kaganovich threw himself into the battle to improve industrial production and enforced rapid collectivization in the Western Ukraine.

In his memoirs Nikita Sergeevich is splendidly malicious and vindictive about Kaganovich. The latter always protected his own backside and put the boot in elsewhere. Patolichev left in August 1947. According to Nikita Sergeevich, Patolichev himself took the initiative because he wanted to escape from Kaganovich – a less convincing reason it would be hard to find! It was not long before Khrushchev himself escaped from Kaganovich. In December 1947 he was reinstated as first party secretary but not in the Kiev posts. A new prime minister also took office. It is uncertain why he weathered the storm but it is another example of his extraordinary ability to escape from tight situations under Stalin.

In December 1949 Khrushchev was promoted to Moscow, becoming a Central Committee secretary and first secretary of the Moscow obkom. Just why Stalin commanded him again to Moscow can only be guessed at. The *vozhd* may have been concerned to clip the wings of Georgy Malenkov and Lavrenty Beria, both of whom had gained from the death of Andrei Zhdanov in August 1948. Stalin launched the notorious 'Leningrad Affair', partly on their advice. Its goal, in reality, was to rid the Party and state apparatus and the second capital of Zhdanovites and replace them with Malenkovites. Another reason may have been the fact that Nikita Sergeevich had become popular in the Ukraine. The master always liked to rotate cadres to ensure that they did not put down roots and thereby lessen his control.

Stalin ensured that there would be friction between Khrushchev and Malenkov by giving the former a wide brief. Malenkov was technically Party secretary for agriculture but knew little about the rural economy. Khrushchev was concerned about reducing the gap between town and country and hit on the idea of amalgamating smaller collective farms into larger units. The number of farms in the Moscow area had been reduced from about 250,000 to 100,000 by 1953. His motivation may have been ideological rather than economic since if small units are inefficient enlarging them will almost certainly make them more inefficient. However, since one of the tenets of Marxian economics is that bigger is better – economies of scale and all that – Khrushchev may have believed that his changes would make the kolkhozes more productive. He placed an article in *Pravda* in 1951 in which he discussed construction problems facing farms and seemed to be promoting the concept of *agrogoroda* or agro-towns. The following day *Pravda* published a note stating that 'due to an editorial oversight' it should have been made clear that 'Comrade

N.S. Khrushchev's article' was for 'discussion only'. Since every reader of *Pravda* knows that 'editorial oversights' do not occur it could only mean that Stalin had intervened. Either the *vozhd* did not like Khrushchev introducing new concepts or someone else, probably Malenkov, had convinced him that his authority was being challenged.

Stalin's intervention could have been fatal for Khrushchev but again he survived the storm. In his memoirs Nikita Sergeevich records that one of the *vozhd*'s practices, in order to judge whether a subordinate was guilty, was to make a serious accusation and then stare straight into the person's eyes. He was looking for any sign of guilt. Khrushchev did not cringe when confronted with an accusation but went on to the offensive. This obviously stood him in good stead on this and other occasions.

Political infighting under high Stalinism could be lethal. Malenkov and Khrushchev locked horns and fought vigorously, with no holds barred, until Khrushchev emerged the victor in February 1955.

At the Nineteenth Party Congress in October 1952, the first congress to be held since 1939, Khrushchev reported on changes in the Party rules. These included changing the Party's name to The Communist Party of the Soviet Union. However, Malenkov presented the main report since Stalin was not well enough. He grasped the opportunity to stick a knife in Khrushchev again by criticizing the 'agro-town' concept. Stalin proposed, through Malenkov, the appointment of a large Presidium. Later he suggested the formation of a Bureau of the Presidium; it did not contain Molotov or Mikoyan but it did include Khrushchev. Then he put forward the idea of an inner group of five – himself, Malenkov, Beria, Bulganin and Khrushchev – to solve the country's most pressing problems. This added substance to the rumours that the *vozhd* was preparing to decapitate the old leadership. All those not in the inner circle were in danger. Some suggested that Stalin was planning to deport all Jews to the inhospitable east.

In his 'Secret Speech' at the Twentieth Party Congress in 1956 Khrushchev accused Stalin of beginning preparations for a wholesale purge. A 'vigilance campaign' was launched after the congress. Then the 'Doctors' Plot', in January 1953, accused mainly Jewish doctors of murdering Andrei Zhdanov and plotting to kill others, including, of course, the *vozhd* himself.

Khrushchev was a member of the charmed inner circle and regularly dined with Stalin at his dacha. This confirmed his standing in the master's entourage but such a position was also loaded with danger. Stalin was a night owl and wined and dined the nights away with his subordinates. Khrushchev was present at the last such binge on 28 February 1953.

> Supper lasted a long time. Stalin referred to it as dinner. We finished about 5 or 6 a.m. – it was usual for those dinners to end at that time … We said goodbye to Comrade Stalin and departed. I remember that when we were in the entrance hall Stalin came out as usual to see us off. He was in jocular mood and joked a lot. He waved his index finger or his fist and prodded me in the stomach, calling me 'Mikola'. He always used the Ukrainian form of my name when he was in good spirits. Well, we left in good spirits too, since nothing had happened during the dinner. Those dinners did not always end on a happy note.[5]

Stalin slept alone behind armour-plated doors which contained panels through which food could be passed. An elaborate system of communication had been evolved. Stalin ordered tea but it could not be brought in until he gave the appropriate signal. It never came and the alarm was raised. The guard commander at the dacha did not feel that he had the authority to burst in, unannounced, on the *vozhd*. He called the Kremlin. The decision rested with Beria and he was in no particular hurry. Either because there is safety in numbers or because no one trusted Beria, it was decided that the four wise men – Stalin's inner circle – would burst in together.

Stalin was eventually found lying on the floor of his dining room. He was put on a couch – something which should not have been done. His personal physician was not available – he was one of those who had been clapped in chains for his alleged part in the 'Doctors' Plot'. The medics finally diagnosed brain haemorrhage, paralysis of the right side and loss of speech. Stalin's fear of assassination and his lack of faith in the medical profession may have cost him his life. Stalin died on 5 March 1953. During his last days his whole demeanour was that of an angry, embittered man. He was only capable of moving his little finger but it was plain what he was trying to convey.

Beria behaved as if he were at a wedding rather than a funeral. For this he earned the undying hatred of Svetlana Alliluyeva, Stalin's daughter, who sees him as the evil man who poisoned her father's mind. Since he was a consummate actor he obviously did not regard it necessary to hide the fact that he was as pleased as punch. Others could shed the crocodile tears. Beria's behaviour could not have been very reassuring to Khrushchev and the others. He was clearly going to be a major player in the post-Stalin power game.

Rising Above Collective Leadership, 1953-57 3

There were no rules or conventions about choosing a new leader. Stalin had ensured that and he had also made sure there was no ready-made successor to step into his shoes. However, since Malenkov had spoken for Stalin at the Nineteenth Party Congress he was seen as the *Kronprinz*, the crown prince. All four wise men – Malenkov, Beria, Bulganin and Khrushchev – wanted to become another Stalin. After all he was the only role model they had. The immediate task for each, however, was to ensure that the others did not succeed. Stalin's last illness gave them time to put together coalitions. To Khrushchev, Beria presented the greatest danger, physically and politically. He set out to ensure that after Stalin's death Lavrenty did not regain control of the security police, then known as the Ministry of State Security (MGB), now the KGB. He talked to Bulganin about this and discovered that he was also uneasy about Beria's aspirations. Then he thought of approaching Malenkov so as to isolate Beria. However, he miscalculated. The master intriguer, Beria, was a move ahead. He and Malenkov had struck a deal. Khrushchev appears not to have anticipated this move but he should have. He

31

should have identified Malenkov as a much more significant player than Bulganin. Perhaps the bad blood between them – encouraged by Stalin – stood in the way. Khrushchev did not think of doing a deal with Beria. He was aware that Lavrenty was very contemptuous of his mental abilities; Beria regarded Khrushchev as a 'moon-faced idiot'!

The first post-Stalin division of power was announced on 7 March. It resulted from the deliberations of the top twenty persons in the Party and the state. No attempt was made to bring all members of the enlarged Presidium and Central Committee of the Party together to decide policy. The new elite decided in the name of the Party and state. It abolished the enlarged Presidium, elected at the Nineteenth Party Congress, and elected a new Presidium of ten. Vyacheslav Molotov, Kliment Voroshilov, Lazar Kaganovich, Anastas Mikoyan and two others joined Malenkov, Beria, Khrushchev and Bulganin.

A major problem was to identify the key political institution. Was it the USSR Council of Ministers or the Party Presidium? Was the prime minister more powerful than the head of the Party? It was not easy to answer the question since there was no post which carried with it the headship of the Party. The position of general secretary had been abolished in 1934 and Stalin thereafter was merely a secretary of the Central Committee. Since Lenin had been prime minister and Stalin had occupied the post since 1941 there was a feeling that whoever was head of government was the key political actor. Of course, he would also sit in the Presidium. Malenkov was nominated prime minister by Beria who, in turn, was proposed as head of the combined Ministries of Internal Affairs (MVD) and State Security (MGB) and deputy prime minister by Malenkov. Khrushchev did not challenge these nominations but in turn suggested Nikolai Bulganin as minister of the armed forces. This was accepted and two deputy ministers, Vasilevsky, the

outgoing minister, and Marshal Georgy Zhukov, were
appointed. Molotov regained the ministry of foreign
affairs. Voroshilov became chairman of the Presidium of
the USSR Supreme Soviet, or head of state. The office
was, however, almost entirely ceremonial. Molotov,
Bulganin, Kaganovich and Mikoyan joined Beria as
deputy prime ministers. The odd man out was Khrushchev. He did not obtain a top government job. He was
released from his Moscow Party posts in order to
concentrate on work in the Central Committee Secretariat. Was he outmanouevred or did he deliberately
choose to concentrate on Party work? No one could
claim that he was unqualified for ministerial duties. After
all he had been prime minister of the Ukraine.

Malenkov acquired all three positions held by Stalin:
prime minister, member of the Presidium and Central
Committee secretary. When the list of secretaries was
published his name, out of alphabetical order, was placed
at the top. He appeared to have put on the mantle of
Stalin. However, he did not inherit the *vozhd*'s power. He
would have to eliminate the others to achieve that.

The first post-Stalin division of power lasted a week.
On 14 March Malenkov left the Party Secretariat but
remained in the Presidium. Since Khrushchev was the
main beneficiary it may be assumed that he was behind
this move. Khrushchev was now the only person who
was in the Secretariat and the Presidium. The Party now
became his power base. As such his goal was to make
the Party the primary institution in the state.

Khrushchev was a member of a collective leadership
but the Soviet political system favours the emergence of
a strong, national leader. The role models were Lenin and
Stalin. Whereas Lenin became leader through his intellectual dominance and tactical political skill Stalin's power
was the result of crushing his political opponents. He
retained his power through ruthlessness and the ability
to inspire fear in his subordinates and the population.

Lenin never was nor never aspired to be the dictator that Stalin became. It was unlikely that the new leader would possess either the intellectual dominance or the power of Stalin.

The nearest thing to Stalin in the leadership was Beria. He was a master of intrigue, refined under Stalin, and was as deadly as a viper. The civil and political police were his power base. He also commanded the border troops and ten MVD divisions. His men also guarded the Kremlin and all military weapons, including nuclear weapons. In the tense, political situation after Stalin's death – *Pravda* appealed to the population not to panic – the leadership had to relax the reins and promise a better tomorrow. Beria was very well informed about domestic and foreign policy. He supported national cadres in non-Russian republics, favoured peasants farming more land for themselves and détente in foreign relations. He sided with the reformers in East Germany and spoke of a neutral Germany.

Beria's colleagues believed that he was planning a *coup*. He was transforming the MVD and reshaping the MGB. He was as suspicious of the others as they were of him. When revolution broke out in East Germany on 17 June 1953 he was dispatched to deal with it. He discovered that a Presidium meeting was to take place the next day. When he phoned he was informed it was merely a routine meeting. Leaving nothing to chance he commandeered a plane and flew back to Moscow straight away.

Khrushchev was the main mover in the conspiracy against Beria which ended with his arrest on 10 July 1953. He already had Bulganin on his side, and by extension the military. However, the key person was Malenkov. Khrushchev eventually won him over, even though he was 'rather nervous'. Then Voroshilov was talked into it. Mikoyan, the great survivor, was more cagey and unwilling to commit himself. Khrushchev and Malenkov worked out the modus operandi of the *coup*. Khrushchev took a gun into the meeting just in case. A major problem was the fact that all personal bodyguards, indeed all personnel concerned with the security of the Party and state elite, took orders from Beria. How was Beria to be arrested and guarded? Who was commander-in-chief of the Soviet armed forces? Eventually Voroshilov, as president, signed an order for Beria's arrest and Marshal Georgy Zhukov was entrusted with the task of carrying it out. Khrushchev made the speech which accused Beria of a whole gamut of crimes, including working for British intelligence in the Caucasus in 1918. Zhukov and ten men waited in an adjoining room for a signal. When Malenkov pressed a button they all rushed in and seized the startled Beria. He was led off and guarded very closely. Then the MVD had to be taken over and this was soon done. The troops guarding the Kremlin were replaced. A purge of Beria's men was set in motion with those resisting being terminated. The whole operation worked like clockwork. Stalin would have been proud of it.

The MVD–MGB apparatus was the greatest barrier to the re-establishment of the dominance of the Communist Party. Now Khrushchev seized the opportunity to promote the claims of the Presidium and the Central Committee. The Council of Ministers was still a powerful institution and Nikita Sergeevich had to be mindful of the fact that the majority of Presidium members were government ministers. Beria helped Khrushchev by discomfiting Malenkov. There was a lot of dirty linen ready to be washed and Beria was keen to get on with the job, even though his sixty-volume testimony revealed his own malodorous behaviour which he seemed to regret. The police chief was known as Stalin's procurer and was wont to pick beauties for himself as well. He had a particular penchant for redheads and liked to frolic in black bedsheets. There was a long list of outraged mothers who did not wish him well. Among the things he freely confessed to were his sexual perversions. It also transpired that he had personally participated in interrogating many prisoners, delighting in inflicting pain.

However, there were too many members in the Presidium and Central Committee who had a vested interest in a selective choice of evidence for the whole sordid story to be told. Nevertheless Khrushchev and others were provided with ammunition which they were to use at a later date. Malenkov's murky past, especially his role in the Leningrad Affair, would be used against him by Khrushchev when the opportune moment arrived.

When sentenced to death Beria turned out to be a coward. He had sent countless innocent people to their deaths and gloated. Guilty, he now prostrated himself and begged for mercy. He was shown none. When facing execution he wanted to make a speech and was gagged lest he spill some more embarrassing beans. Soldiers competed eagerly with one another to be members of the execution squad.

Condemning Beria and his henchmen for crimes which were part and parcel of the Soviet system under Stalin was a risky business. Every man in the leadership – there were no women – was explicitly or implicitly involved in some of the crimes. There was the vast Gulag system, about which Aleksandr Solzhenitsyn has written so evocatively and movingly, with its hundreds of camps and millions of prisoners, all under the supervision of the MVD. Many of the prisoners were innocent. How were their cases to be reviewed without undermining the integrity of the state? A state built on coercion, fear and lies risked disintegration when it conceded the truth about itself. The problem of how much of the truth to tell was never resolved by Khrushchev. Gorbachev was more courageous but shattered the state.

A cautious beginning was made to rehabilitate the innocent. But it only affected the elite, their families and friends. About a thousand had been rehabilitated (some posthumously) by the end of 1953. One of those who returned to Moscow was Lyubov Khrushcheva, the widow of Leonid, Khrushchev's son. He had died in aerial combat in 1943 near Voronezh. He was never found as his plane had disappeared into a bog. Lyubov was arrested and condemned as a Swedish spy. Another was Molotov's wife and the accusations that she had spied for the US and Israel (she was a Jewess) were dismissed. In normal circumstances, if the wife of a former minister of foreign affairs had been found guilty of spying for the 'great imperialist enemy', the US, it would also have meant the end of his career. Perhaps Stalin wanted to have Molotov even deeper in his thrall. He played cat and mouse with Molotov. On one occasion he told him that he had been reliably informed that he was a Jew. Molotov could get out about one sentence before he began to stutter. On this occasion he fluently replied: 'Oh, no, Comrade Stalin, you have been misinformed.' Whereupon Stalin countered: 'Vyacheslav Mikhailovich, I would think it over, if I were you!'

Beria's removal ended the first round of the battle for supreme power. Now the contest was between Malenkov and his allies, and Khrushchev and his allies. Malenkov's power base was the government and Khrushchev's the Party.

The latter's common touch revealed itself quickly. Stalin had transformed the Kremlin into his own fortress. No one was allowed into it without a special pass. Even photographing it was prohibited. Towards the end of 1953 it was reopened to the public; this time all that was needed was a ticket. A New Year's Eve ball was inaugurated for young people and Christmas trees put up for the children. It became quite an event under Khrushchev.

Control over the civil and political police after Beria's demise was of supreme importance. The Ministry of Internal Affairs (MVD) was to be responsible for investigating all civil and criminal offences and a newly constituted Committee of State Security (KGB) was to be responsible for state security, at home and abroad. The latter was to continue to guard all state and Party personnel. A subtle change was engineered here. Whereas previously all instructions derived from Beria, now the bodyguards were to receive their orders from the person they were guarding. Khrushchev managed to influence the selection of the first head of the KGB, General Ivan Serov. He knew him well from the Ukraine where he had been People's Commissar for Internal Affairs. Although Khrushchev trusted him – 'I thought and still think him to be an honest man where the Party is concerned. And if there is something "on him", as is the case with all Chekists, so to speak, well, he was in that respect a victim of the general policy that Stalin pursued'[1] – Serov had an unsavoury reputation. When he preceded Khrushchev and Bulganin to London in 1956 the popular press savaged him and he was promptly recalled. Khrushchev did not know Kruglov, the MVD head. Revealingly this meant that Nikita Sergeevich did not trust him. The procurator-general became the supreme law enforcement officer in the Soviet Union and his counterpart at republican and lower levels, all of whom were subordinate to him. The notorious Special Boards, under which the political police had had the power to sentence defendants in their absence, were phased out. Of course, all this did not transform the Soviet Union into the Rechtsstaat where the rule of law prevailed. However, it did begin the process of the rehabilitation of socialist law. Socialist legality would still be defined by the supreme Party organ, the Presidium.

Khrushchev, in order to outgun Malenkov, deployed refined Stalinist skills. The rules of the game had been set by the master but Nikita Sergeevich revealed greater daring, enthusiasm and originality than his opponent. An important policy area was personnel. The Soviet system is based on the *nomenklatura*, which is both a list of all key positions and available individuals to fill them. Each official attempts to build up a 'tail' of loyal henchmen. As the official moves upwards many of the subordinates move up as well. They, in turn, grow 'tails'. The upwardly mobile politician is like a growing tree. Since the other members of the state and Party elite were trying simultaneously to expand their 'tails', considerable skill is needed to place one's men and a few women in positions of minor and major influence. Nikita Sergeevich started with a great advantage: he was *de facto* head of the Party. This was not enough. He had to promote policies which promised to move the country forward politically, economically and socially. Then there was the need to strike tactical political coalitions to downgrade gradually political opponents. Above all he needed some luck. If Malenkov's economic policies were brilliantly successful then Khrushchev might not climb to the top of the political pole. Needless to say he was not going to do anything to make Georgy Maksimilianovich a political or economic success.

It took Khrushchev until February 1955, when Malenkov resigned as prime minister, to get the better of his arch rival. After Stalin's death Khrushchev was just another member of the political elite, but he soon became *de facto* Party leader. Then he became *primus inter pares* (first among equals) when Malenkov gave up his government post but did not become a strong, national leader until July 1957. Technically he was only Party leader in July 1957 and in order to become a strong, national leader he needed a great office of state. Although he took over as prime minister, replacing Nikolai Bulganin in March 1958, he had been in reality head of government since the summer of 1957. Bulganin had been a member of the Anti-Party group defeated by Khrushchev and had been permitted to stay in office mainly for appearances' sake. The Yugoslav ambassador, Micunovic, relates that he advised against the demotion of Bulganin in July 1957.

Those abroad might construe such a move by Khrushchev as proof that he was just another Stalinist hood. By the summer of 1958 Khrushchev had emulated his mentor, Stalin. It had taken him five years to do so, the same period Iosif Vissarionovich had needed. Stalin's task had been immeasurably more difficult. Nikita Sergeevich had not had to outmanoeuvre such hugely talented comrades as Trotsky and Bukharin. It requires an enormous stretch of the imagination to conceive of Nikita Sergeevich getting the better of those two, given the fact that he did not regard killing one's political opponents as one of the rules of the game. Stalin had done Khrushchev a favour. All the clever men had been eliminated from the top echelons of political power and no new ones allowed to take their place. One can speak of the law of diminishing brain power. The brilliant Lenin was followed by the crafty Stalin who killed intellectual debate at the top. Then came Khrushchev who only had a limited grasp of Marxism. He was followed by Brezhnev, who preferred flattery to hard thinking. Andropov was never well enough to make an impact. The depths were plummeted by the election of Chernenko. Perhaps one should not be too harsh on him. He could hardly speak. The arrival of Gorbachev was the exception which proved the rule. The limited intellectual ability of so many of the leadership had a catastrophic effect on the way the country was run. Moreover the expansion of education had produced many highly talented, educated people in every walk of life. There could not be a debate between leaders and led since the leadership could not sustain such a debate. The result was a loss of political authority by the leaders. Another by-product was that violent quarrels were certain to break out between the intelligentsia and the guardians of political orthodoxy. The latter's views reflected the past and favoured the status quo whereas creative minds wanted to move forward. Khrushchev was to be caught up in this struggle and to side with the orthodox officials.

Only in retirement did he see the error of his ways.

Khrushchev chose not to apply one of the rules of the political game at which Stalin was a past master: coercion. Nikita Sergeevich abjured the use of force for political gain. This made his task in the race to become a strong, national leader much more difficult. As late as July 1957 his defeated opponents expected to suffer physically as well as politically for their defeat. It also made his hold on power less secure since opponents became more bold in opposing those policies they deemed inimical to their interests.

What are the rules of the political game in the USSR and how did the fertile mind of Khrushchev apply them?

Being head of the Central Committee (CC) Secretariat meant he could place his nominees in key Party posts and infiltrate the government network, where he was weak. *De facto* head in March, he became *de jure* head in September 1953 when he was elected first secretary of the CC of the Communist Party of the Soviet Union. This was a new post since Stalin had been general secretary until 1934. Clearly the new title was to stress the break with the past. Brezhnev had himself renamed general secretary in 1966.

There were five main types of official Khrushchev sought to make part of his 'tail':

1) those who had served successfully under him in the Ukraine and Moscow;
2) those whose patrons had lost ground in the leadership struggle, such as Beria's men after July 1953 and Malenkov's entourage after February 1955;
3) those who had been Stalin's men until his death and who had then lost out to the aspirations of Malenkov, Beria, Molotov and their 'tails';
4) those who had been the losers in the factional infighting of the later Stalin era, e.g. the Leningrad Affair;

5) bright, capable, young officials who could be promoted over the heads of their superiors.

The group which did best after Khrushchev entered the Secretariat were, not surprisingly, those who had been in his team in the Ukraine and Moscow. Many of them became first Party secretaries at *oblast* and *krai* levels and others moved into the central Party apparatus in Moscow. Recruits from groups 3 and 4 promised to be loyal since they were resentful of Beria and Malenkov. One informed estimate is that by the time of the Twentieth Party Congress in February 1956 Khrushchev's Ukrainian and Moscow supporters and the others listed above constituted about a third of the full members of the CC. By the end of 1957, after consolidating his victory over the Anti-Party group, Nikita Sergeevich's team from the above groups made up the overwhelming majority of full CC members.

Besides cultivating his 'tail' in Moscow, Khrushchev was quietly doing the same in the republican communist parties. Each of the republics had its own party with the exception of the Russian Federation. Republican parties were subject to close control from the centre. It is reasonable to assume that Khrushchev's orbit of patronage took in republican, *oblast* and *krai* government leaders, top-flight police officers and officials in agricultural ministries. However, the majority of senior posts in the central government apparatus were still beyond his reach.

The Stalinist command economy, now referred to as the administrative-command system, had concentrated great power in the central governmental ministries. Since Nikita Sergeevich's main Presidium opponents had their power bases in these ministries there was little he could do to dislodge them if the economy continued to function as before. He hit on the idea that if economic decision-making could be more decentralized it would help him in two ways. It would undermine the political bases of his challengers and since there was no intention to go over to a market economy, an organization would be needed to allocate resources, control, co-ordinate and resolve the conflicts which would inevitably arise. The natural organization to perform this function was the Party. Its apparatus would gradually become more influential than that of the government. The *nomenklatura* system would facilitate the placing of the right people in government and local authority or soviet jobs.

Given the fact that Khrushchev's political opponents must have been aware of the long-term objective of the devolution of economic decision-making, he was surprisingly successful. In 1954–55 about 11,000 enterprises were transferred from central to republican control. In May 1955 many major planning and financial decisions, hitherto taken in the capital, were devolved to republican governments. In May 1956 factories run by twelve central governmental ministries were placed under the jurisdiction of republican bodies. Then in May 1957 over a hundred Councils of the National Economy (*sovnarkhozy*) were established, thereby eliminating the central economic ministries. Ministries involved in the defence sector were exempt.

It was only when Khrushchev pushed through the *sovnarkhoz* reform that the Presidium majority revolted. They had to challenge the brash innovator since it was quite clear that he wished to push them aside politically. Little that Nikita Sergeevich ever did was very subtle.

Khrushchev needed policy issues to challenge Malenkov effectively. The latter (and Beria) had launched the New Course after Stalin's death. Its goal was to convince people that things would get better and thereby lessen the odds of civil strife. This was vital during a period of weak collective rule. The New Course switched resources from heavy industry to light and favoured the intensification of agriculture. What is now called democratization

– more discussion at grassroots but firm central control – was encouraged. The East European communist states were encouraged to follow suit. For instance, the hardline East German Communist Party, the SED, under its leader Walter Ulbricht, was sharply criticized at a joint conference with the Communist Party of the Soviet Union after Stalin's funeral. Ulbricht did not heed the criticism and his policies led to the uprising of 17 June 1953. Some of the blame for this was heaped on Beria.

Agriculture: the Virgin Lands

Domestically Khrushchev had to respond to Malenkov's economic initiatives. Malenkov was stronger on industrial than on rural affairs. Fortunately for Nikita Sergeevich *his* strengths were the other way round. At the Nineteenth Party Congress in 1952 Malenkov had given a hostage to fortune by declaring that the grain problem had 'in the main been solved'. This was based on estimated yields of standing corn, called the biological yield, and were about one-third higher than what actually ended up in the barn. It was child's play for Khrushchev to demonstrate that Malenkov was wrong. Everyone agreed that a rapid expansion of grain output was vital. This in turn would permit the animal population to rise, thus providing more meat and milk products. He launched his policy in September 1953 and it amounted to a call for extensive agriculture – sow more, harvest more, eat more. But how was he to obtain control of the implementation of this policy? The central agricultural ministries were administered by his opponents and the farms – kolkhozes or collective farms, and sovkhozes or state farms – were not subordinate to him. The most effective way of gaining control of agriculture would be to make the Party official lord of the countryside. In September he managed to make a *raion* Party secretary and his assistants, centred in the Machine Tractor Stations (MTS), the chief supervisors of the implementation of agrarian policy in the kolkhozes. In those days farms did not possess their own machinery since there was not enough to go round. The agricultural departments of the *raion* soviets were abolished. This weakened the links between the farms and the agricultural agencies and central government. Information about the rural sector gradually fell within the orbit of the Party. This made Khrushchev the best informed person on agriculture. The reform was an astute political move but was of questionable economic value. This arrangement remained until 1958 when the MTS were abolished and machinery sold, or more accurately offloaded on to the farms. There was no longer any need to run agriculture from the MTS since by then the *raion* first Party secretary had established his authority. Another reason was that in 1958 Khrushchev became prime minister and hence head of the governmental administration.

Since agricultural output in 1953 grew only by 2.5 per cent (industrial production claimed a 12 per cent rise) there was an urgent need to increase food output. Khrushchev knew that there were millions of hectares of virgin and idle land (which had recently been cultivated and then abandoned) throughout the country. However, much of it was marginal and in dry farming zones where different techniques are needed to preserve the fertility of the soil. In February 1954 hundreds of thousands of Komsomol (young communist) members from Moscow city and *oblast* assembled in the capital. Khrushchev and the minister of agriculture, I.A. Benediktov, appealed to the young people to take part in the opening up of virgin and idle land. Since there would be no creature comforts in West Siberia, north Kazakhstan, the Urals and the north Caucasus, the imagination of the young people had to be fired. The older generation would prefer to stay at home. There were doubters on the Party Presidium, especially Molotov, who preferred intensification.

Khrushchev argued that that would be expensive and only produce results slowly. His initiative would be cheaper – recouping costs within two to three years, one of his favourite expressions – and would produce results very quickly. Perhaps his political opponents thought they were giving him enough rope to hang himself. He very nearly did.

The Kazakhs were not enamoured of the idea at all. North Kazakhstan was used to graze livestock. Ploughing it up would bring in a flood of Russians, Ukrainians and others, thus making the Kazakhs, a minority in their own republic, even worse off. Khrushchev sacked the Kazakh Party leadership and installed his own men. The comrade chosen to be second secretary was Leonid Ilich Brezhnev. He was later to become first secretary. By the end of February thousands of young enthusiasts were on their way to Siberia and Kazahkstan. Most of them had no experience of agriculture, let alone dry farming, and they had no tools. They were to come straight from the factories. Only the most perfunctory of surveys had been carried out in Kazakhstan. The need for more food was so urgent that willpower was most highly regarded. It was reminiscent of the 1930s.

A CC plenum in February 1954 approved Khrushchev's proposal to plough up 13 million hectares of virgin land which was expected to yield 20 million tonnes of grain in 1955. This was certainly ambitious but Nikita Sergeevich was a conviction politician and he was convinced the Virgin Lands were the new Eldorado for the Soviet Union. State farms had to be set up since no one at present farmed there. A CC plenum in May 1954 heard another wonder solution: the cultivation of maize. This was to solve the fodder problem at a stroke. He did not pretend that the average peasant would agree with him so he asked for sowing of maize to be made mandatory everywhere. Coercion should be used wherever necessary. After all peasants had refused to believe that potatoes were good for them in the eighteenth century! It was judged politic not to publish the bit about coercion. His passion for maize – it is a valuable crop in parts of the Ukraine but rarely ripens elsewhere – earned him the sobriquet Comrade Kukuruznik (from the Russian word for maize, *kukuruza*). It was not intended to be complimentary. So keen was he on the crop that he grew it at his dacha in Moscow.

Agricultural production was officially stated to have increased by only 3 per cent. The food problem had still to be solved. Another CC plenum in January 1955 launched a livestock plan but procurement prices – what the state paid the farms – were raised. In March 1955 the minister of state farms (most of the Virgin Lands came under this ministry) was sacked and replaced by Benediktov, the minister of agriculture. The new minister of agriculture was Vladimir Matskevich, whom Khrushchev knew from his Ukrainian days. Matskevich was also an animal husbandry specialist.

Khrushchev continued his policy of amalgamating kolkhozes. Between 1953 and 1958 their number dropped from over 90,000 to under 70,000 and declined rapidly thereafter. There were two reasons for this. Larger units were regarded as more efficient and in 1953 very few farms had a primary Party organization. Over 20,000 technical specialists and Party members were transferred from the cities to the MTS and farms. As a result over 90 per cent of kolkhoz chairmen by 1958 were communists and the average kolkhoz had a primary Party organization of about twenty members. Khrushchev had created the Party network in the countryside which could be used as an instrument of change. It was appreciated there had to be a material incentive to raise production. By the end of the Stalin era most farms operated at a loss since procurement prices had hardly moved since 1928. Procurement prices between June 1953 and 1957 almost trebled. The policy of expanding the sown area was pursued vigorously. Over the years 1954–60 a staggering 41.8 million hectares of virgin and idle land were ploughed with West Siberia and north Kazakhstan accounting for three-quarters. However, in 1960 the increase in the sown area was only 30 million hectares. State procurements of grain rose by almost 50 per cent annually between 1954–63 with most of the increase coming from the Virgin Lands. However, the cost of producing this extra grain was very high. The Soviet Union refused to import grain for domestic consumption before 1963. Hence grain at any price was preferable to starving.

How did it come about that Khrushchev was able to play such an innovative role in agriculture? After all the rural economy came within the brief of the government. He was also able to influence industrial decision-making. After Stalin's death it was not clear where the centre of legitimacy in the Soviet state lay. Nikita Sergeevich skilfully argued that the Party Central Committee was the key institution. Between March 1953 and July 1957 the CC played a role reminiscent of that in the latter part of the 1920s. After Lenin's death Stalin enjoyed more support in the CC than in the Politburo. Hence he concentrated debate in the CC and appealed to it if Politburo members rejected his policies. However, with Stalin in the saddle after 1929, the CC declined rapidly in influence. During the last six years of Stalin's life it only met in plenary session twice. Membership merely confirmed a comrade's standing. In March 1953 the government was clearly the leading organ of the state but with Malenkov head of both the government and the Party the relationship between the two was unclear. When Khrushchev became *de facto* head of the Party apparatus one can assume that he sedulously propagated the view that all key decisions should be debated and confirmed by a CC plenum. According to the Party rules, after all, the CC is the supreme Party body. Nikita Sergeevich had his way and the practice evolved that every major shift in power among the elite should be confirmed by a CC plenum. The first division of power after Stalin's death, Beria's arrest, Khrushchev's appointment as first secretary and Malenkov's dismissal as prime minister were all endorsed by a CC plenum.

Since Nikita Sergeevich had no governmental office the only way he could propagate his agricultural views was by convening a CC plenum. Being head of the Secretariat made this a simple task. Another tactic was to address a memorandum to Presidium members. Only those who were present knew exactly what Khrushchev was proposing. Most of his speeches at this time were only published in 1962. His use of the CC plenum transformed it into a body which participated in the formation of policy. Enormous publicity attended the meetings and the proceedings were later published, a major innovation. CC plenums took place in September 1953 to launch Khrushchev's agricultural policy, in February 1954 to begin the Virgin Lands campaign, in June 1954, again on the Virgin Lands, and in January 1955 to propagate his livestock policy.

Foreign policy

The resurgence of the influence of the Party permitted Khrushchev to play a role in foreign affairs. Relations between the Soviet Union and other socialist countries are conducted at Party level. Nikita Sergeevich seized the opportunity to upgrade the role of the Party and to push Molotov, the minister of foreign affairs, aside. Stalin left a legacy of hostility but an armistice was signed in July 1953 in Korea. In 1954 an agreement was signed which achieved a ceasefire and partitioned Vietnam. Relations with the People's Republic of China were not very fraternal. Mao Zedong and Stalin had never hit it off since the latter had tried to turn China into another satellite. Credits and technical aid were extended to Beijing and this prepared the way for an official visit in late September 1954. The Soviet delegation was headed by Khrushchev, Bulganin, as prime minister, and Mikoyan. Molotov was left at home. Nikita Sergeevich and Mao had many conversations. Some of them were held lounging around a swimming pool. This must have been an appalling sight with the mountains of flesh on view! Anyway the wily Mao bamboozled Khrushchev. The latter records that many of Mao's statements were so complex that they were opaque in the extreme. Others were so mundane that they amounted to the obvious. Mao must have been very pleased with the negotiations since he got practically all he asked for. Port Arthur was to be returned to China and the Soviets were to hand over their share of jointly owned concerns. A host of specialists from the Soviet Union, and eventually Eastern Europe, were to be sent to build socialism there. It was all give and no take. No wonder Molotov had been left at home.

Yugoslavia was to prove a more daunting test. Expelled from the socialist commonwealth in 1948 the conventional wisdom was that Tito's regime was a 'military-fascist dictatorship'. No one had been able to come up with anything more insulting. Nice things were now written in *Pravda* about the Yugoslav–Soviet relationship and Tass described relations as 'cordial' in November 1954 after the Soviet leadership had turned up to celebrate Independence Day at the Yugoslav embassy in Moscow. Just how cordial relations were was demonstrated when Khrushchev, Bulganin, Mikoyan and Dmitri Shepilov flew to Belgrade in May 1955 to mend fences. Again Molotov was left at home. The Soviet delegation was thankful to set foot on terra firma since their pilot did not know the airport and found landing difficult. Tito welcomed them and then switched the microphones off so that few could hear Nikita Sergeevich. Tito also gave orders that Khrushchev's words were not to be translated. The latter, predictably, heaped all the blame for the break in relations on Beria. Tito was not impressed. At the subsequent reception at the White Palace the elegant Yugoslav leaders and their ladies in Parisian dresses looked down their noses at the ill-dressed Soviets. At the return reception Nikita Sergeevich got carried away and imbibed too much.

> He had to be carried out between rows of diplomats and other guests on the arms of Tito and Rankovic, with his feet sketching out the motions of walking without ever touching the ground.[2]

Sir Frank Roberts, as British Ambassador, observed the visit. Khrushchev's tackling of the Yugoslav problem was typical of his approach to so many of the problems he thought he could solve.

> He started with a brainwave, calling for rapid action alien to the thought processes of his more plodding colleagues and running risks of failure and even humiliation, but which, if successful, could bring big dividends and realise important policy objectives. His impulsive handling of the situation was clumsy and counter-productive, but he then retrieved from the apparent wreck enough of his original purpose to justify the enterprise.[3]

Nikita Sergeevich, who always regarded the Party as the core of political life, wanted to restore inter-Party relations with the Yugoslavs and to welcome them back as the prodigal son to the socialist commonwealth. Tito had no intention of conceding the primacy of the CPSU – Nikita Sergeevich always insisted that his party knew best. The Yugoslavs were willing to restore inter-state relations. They were leaders of the non-aligned movement and were to lean in the direction of the Soviet Union from time to time. For instance, Tito sided with

Khrushchev over the Hungarian Revolution in 1956. Khrushchev's high-risk strategy began to pay other dividends. The West began to perceive that the Stalinist mould was being broken and that it could negotiate seriously with the Soviet leaders. One of the first fruits of this was the Austrian Peace Treaty in May 1955. Molotov, predictably, objected to the Soviet concessions. Soviet troops left the country voluntarily, the first time this had happened since the war, and Austria became a neutral country. This indicated a change in Soviet thinking. Hitherto the Soviets had hoped that partitioned Austria and Germany would fall into their lap. Now they perceived that this was not going to happen and left Austria. They did make one gain, however. Since Austria became neutral NATO troops and equipment could not pass through Austria en route to Italy. They would have to cross via France.

The Warsaw Pact, the Socialist riposte to NATO, also came into being in May 1955. The original draft, prepared by Molotov, did not contain Yugoslavia, of course. But it also omitted Albania and the German Democratic Republic. The reason for omitting Albania was that it was 'far away' and had no common frontier with the Soviet Union. As for the GDR, Molotov posed the question: 'Why should we fight with the West over the GDR?' Khrushchev pointed out that if these two countries were omitted it would give the West *carte blanche* to take them over. This view prevailed.

The first summit meeting since Potsdam took place in Geneva in July 1955. Khrushchev, Bulganin, Molotov and Marshal Zhukov represented the Soviet Union but Molotov did not participate in any of the major discussions. Many issues were discussed, especially Germany, but no agreement was reached. The communiqué stated that the American, British, French and Soviet foreign ministers would continue negotiations afterwards. It also stated that all-German elections were possible. The Americans took this too literally and were very annoyed when Khrushchev reassured Walter Ulbricht in East Berlin that this would only happen with GDR consent, which, of course, would not be forthcoming. The East German leadership felt weak and always lived in fear of the Soviets and Americans doing a deal over their heads. Soviet policy towards Germany thus changed and for the first time it was stated that the 'socialist achievements' of the GDR had to be preserved. Later Khrushchev was to inform a French delegation that the reality of 17 million East Germans building socialism was preferable to an all-German neutral state. At Geneva Nikita Sergeevich got on best with the French and delighted in calling Edgar Faure, the head of the delegation, Edgar Fedorovich.

In a 'strictly secret' letter to Walter Ulbricht dated 14 July 1955, Khrushchev informed him that the decision had been taken to release all the German prisoners of war and civilians who were still being held in the Soviet Union. They included those who were still classified as war criminals. This was a prelude to negotiations to establish diplomatic relations with Bonn. The negotiations, in September 1955, were hard and threatened to collapse over the question of repatriation. It is now clear that this was a negotiating ploy by Khrushchev to ensure that Chancellor Konrad Adenauer agreed to diplomatic relations being established. The chief goal of the Soviets was to establish beneficial trade links with Bonn. Adenauer, in turn, tried to 'buy' the GDR from Moscow by offering generous credits and reparations. Khrushchev resisted the temptation. He remarked: 'Once you start retreating, it's difficult to stop'. The prisoners were released a week after Adenauer's visit. To camouflage the concession Nikita Sergeevich claimed that it had only been taken at the urging of the GDR. The above letter reveals the claim to be false. The Soviet people caught the flavour of the negotiations by reading the speeches in the press. This was another innovation by Khrushchev.

The United States' efforts in 1954–55 to widen the ring of containment around the Soviet Union by enlisting countries on its southern periphery – Pakistan, Iran and Iraq – caused great apprehension in Moscow. The hostile reception US policy received in the emerging Third World encouraged the Soviets to cultivate countries in that region.

In October 1955 U Nu, the Burmese leader, visited Moscow and the following month Khrushchev and Bulganin travelled to Burma, India and Afghanistan. Nehru had paid an official visit to the Soviet Union in 1954. The Indian sojourn was a triumphal progress but accompanied by physical danger. So great was the crush on one occasion that their official car was taken to pieces by the crowd. They were then passed overhead by their security guards to safety. Their tour was headline news throughout the world.

Soviet standing in the world was given a massive boost in December 1955 when it exploded its second massive thermo-nuclear device at high altitude. Moscow had a transportable hydrogen bomb which was bigger than any American weapon of destruction. The Soviet Union was now in the big league. Among those who were elected Academicians was the 'father' of the Soviet bomb, Andrei Sakharov. Nikita Sergeevich was fascinated by rockets and weaponry and took an almost childish delight in discussing their design and capabilities with scientists and engineers. Rather like a child with a new toy he could not resist boasting about his rockets being better than anyone else's. This was later to have unfortunate side effects and to trigger an escalation in the arms race as the Americans took his braggadocio seriously.

The Khrushchev–Bulganin double act reached London in April 1956. (They were known as B & K there.) By now the relationship had to establish who was top dog. When a British reporter naïvely took the prime minister as the senior partner and posed a serious question, Khrushchev answered it. They had something to live down since General Serov, head of the KGB, sent ahead to arrange security, had had to beat a hasty retreat after being mangled by the British popular press. Another fatality of the visit was Commander Crabbe, who had attempted to inspect the hull of the ship, *Ordzhonikidze*, which had brought the Soviet guests to England. He disappeared and his body was later found floating nearby. Khrushchev found the trip enormously stimulating and met, among others, the Queen and Sir Winston Churchill. When he talked about the process of change being very complex, the British veteran advised the Soviet leader to be bold. 'Any delay could result in the most serious consequences. It is like crossing a precipice. One may leap over it, if one has sufficient strength, but never in two jumps.'

In an attempt to forge a new 'popular front' against NATO and American influence Nikita Sergeevich met Labour Party leaders. By now Khrushchev had the reputation of being 'The Mouth' and he lived up to his sobriquet. He bragged about the Soviet hydrogen bomb and hinted about a Moscow–Bonn axis turned against the Western powers. There were elements in the Labour Party which might have taken him up, but not Hugh Gaitskell. He demanded that political prisoners in the Soviet Union and Eastern Europe be released. This stung Khrushchev and he retorted that if 'this was British socialism, he preferred to be a Tory'.

Khrushchev had by the summer of 1956 evolved 'new political thinking' in foreign policy. Its core was peaceful co-existence. This doctrine did not originate with Khrushchev but he developed it and gave it new nuances. It was now possible because of the growing strength of the world socialist system. Nikita Sergeevich was convinced that socialism was going to win worldwide but through peaceful competition. Wars were no longer inevitable – this had been stated as early as 1952. Present policy consisted of improving relations with the great powers;

the elimination of sources of conflict which could lead to war; the amelioration of relations with several European states; exploration of new ways of solving problems such as European security, disarmament and the German problem; rapprochement with all countries in the search to preserve peace; expanded contacts with leaders and exchange of delegations. Much of this anticipated Gorbachev's foreign policy. Khrushchev was very optimistic about the prospects of putting together a coalition of the left to join communists in the struggle against war and reaction. He was keen to push the concept of a Treaty of Friendship and Cooperation with the United States.

The Twentieth Party Congress and its aftermath

The congress was announced well in advance, in June 1955. Hence it became a focal point for all those seeking change. Open trials of Beria's sidekicks took place throughout 1954–55 and made an enormous impact. However, perhaps only 10,000 had been freed from the labour camps and rehabilitated and others posthumously. Most of those affected were Party apparatchiks. The ordinary people, and there were millions of them in the gulag, went on suffering. Discipline began to break down in some of the camps but repression was ferocious. Nevertheless the atmosphere was changing. Commissions had been set up to investigate the crimes of the Stalin era so more and more material was accumulating. Khrushchev wanted a section of the CC's report to the congress to be devoted to the cult of personality and its consequences. Molotov, Malenkov, Kaganovich and Voroshilov resolutely opposed this. 'This is not to be your personal report but is that of the entire CC,' they retorted. Nikita Sergeevich also proposed that some Party officials, now rehabilitated, should address the delegates. This found no favour as it threatened many in the Party elite.

The congress opened on 14 February 1956. The official reports painted an optimistic picture. The economy was expanding with agriculture surging ahead: 1955 was a record year and 1956 was to turn out even better. Housing – especially the five-storey blocks without any lifts – was experiencing a boom and there were more consumer goods and services on offer. The outlook in foreign policy was very good. The Soviet Union had abandoned Stalin's 'two camp' theory whereby all those not with the USSR were deemed against it. It was possible to conclude alliances with non-socialist states for tactical reasons. Khrushchev also conceded that there were many roads to socialism. Workers might win a majority in parliament and proclaim the victory of socialism in that way. Things had changed! The name of Stalin was not mentioned but there were references to 'Beria's gang'.

How was Khrushchev to raise the issue of Stalin's crimes? One way would be to speak as an ordinary delegate from the floor. That made many 'Stalinists' nervous since the whole world would hear the words and their careers would be over. Eventually it was agreed that he deliver a report in the name of the CC, not to an open but to a closed session, after the new CC had been elected. There was to be no discussion of this report. Mikoyan prepared the way for Khrushchev. He criticized Stalin directly. 'For twenty years we had no collective leadership: the cult of personality flourished.' He stated that some of Stalin's pronouncements had proved erroneous.

The 'Secret Speech' is a misnomer. It was delivered to congress delegates and others specially invited. Interestingly not enough guests from ruling communist and non-communist parties were invited. They were briefed afterwards but only in Russian. The revelations contained in it ensured that it would become a worldwide sensation immediately. The report is a violent denunciation of Stalin and all his works between 1934 and 1953. It does not touch on the early years and accepts that rapid industrialization and enforced collectivization were necessary. It is a paean of praise to the Party and a cry of anguish at its suffering. Ordinary mortals are ignored. One of the reasons for its shortcomings is the haste with which it was put together. Nikita Sergeevich never wrote a speech in his life. He found writing hard and made many mistakes. (Russian, grammatically and orthographically, is a difficult language.) He usually dictated a rough outline, then used that as a basis, adding and deleting as new ideas occurred to him. He had the evidence of the various commissions at his disposal and he had talked to many of the Party victims who had returned from the gulag. Moreover he found it very difficult to keep to a prepared text at the rostrum and extemporized a lot.

What he had to say shocked, amazed and stunned his audience. Their whole world was demolished in front of their eyes. They had worshipped Stalin as a father and infallible leader. They were told that he had originated the purges, tortured victims, including members of the Politburo, that he was responsible for the early defeats of the war, that all the economic ills and failures in foreign policy were his fault, that he had sedulously cultivated his personality cult and that he had falsified Party history and his own biography. Khrushchev got carried away in his wreaking of vengeance on Stalin. One delegate was so shocked by the revelations that she was unable to raise her arm to vote acceptance of the report.

Khrushchev took an immense personal risk in delivering the speech. Had Molotov, Malenkov and Kaganovich, for instance, known the full details of what he was going to say they would undoubtedly have tried to block him. Had the speech been delivered to the leading luminaries of the communist world outside the Soviet Union there would have been howls of protest. For instance, Mao Zedong never forgave Khrushchev for not revealing to him what he intended to do beforehand.

So why did he do it? After all there was blood on his hands also. Why had he and others not put a brake on Stalin's crimes?

One explanation would be that his purpose was to liberate Party officials from the fear of repression. Under Stalin no one was safe and the further away from Moscow the better. Promotion was not welcomed by many. Nikita Sergeevich felt that if the Party could become an efficient mechanism, stripped of the brutal abuse of power by any individual, it could transform the country and the world. The Secret Speech concentrates on the crimes committed against Party cadres. It does not exonerate those who lost in the power struggles against Stalin. Other models of socialism remained, as before, illegitimate.

Another view would be that the demolition of Stalin was a tactical move in the power struggle at the top of the Party and state. By assaulting Stalin, Nikita Sergeevich was undermining the credibility of Molotov, Malenkov, Kaganovich and others who had worked closely with him. They now had a choice: switch to his side or risk being banished with Stalin.

The liberation of millions from the camps was a great and good act, indeed a 'miracle', in Solzhenitsyn's view. It was due less to political calculation than to a 'movement of the heart' of Khrushchev. He had broken the spell of the Stalin era and was capable of repenting and expiating his crimes.

The report was distributed to Party organizations and read out at meetings. No questions were permitted. It was not welcomed in many quarters, especially in Georgia, Stalin's native republic. The report exploded the myth of the infallibility of the Party. It undermined its authority but in order to survive it had to become more democratic. One of its weaknesses was its lack of contact with ordinary members. Policy and ideological innovation had always been decided at the top and then handed down. Khrushchev, unwittingly, made the Party a less effective weapon in the battle for change.

The Twentieth Party Congress sharpened conflict within the Presidium and the CC. Two new full members were added to the Presidium, Andrei Kirichenko and Mikhail Suslov. Both were to play important roles later. No one was dropped. Among the new candidate members were Leonid Brezhnev, Marshal Georgy Zhukov and Dmitri Shepilov, all Khrushchev men. Shepilov was to replace Molotov as foreign minister in June 1956. The composition of the CC changed substantially. Almost half of those elected in 1952 were dropped and fifty-four new names added. Khrushchev's influence here was evident.

The denunciation of Stalin led to the freeing of millions of political prisoners. Their stories horrified many and added to the groundswell for a more democratic and just society. Communists had their Party membership restored and were to be given priority in seeking accommodation, work and, if necessary, pensions. Khrushchev did not back away from confessing that he bore some responsibility for Stalin's crimes. At a meeting after the congress he received a note asking him why he had allowed such crimes to be committed. He asked who had written the note. There was only silence. 'The person who wrote this note is frightened. Well, we were frightened to stand up to Stalin.' At least Khrushchev was honest.

Writers and other intellectuals began demanding greater freedom for creativity and the punishment of those who had repressed them. Daring new works appeared and Ilya Ehrenburg's novel *The Thaw* was published and its title symbolizes the period. There was a remarkable flowering of poetry and many who have since become household names made their appearance: Evgeny Evtushenko, Voznesensky, Okudzhava and Akhmaduļlina, for instance. Evtushenko has described those heady days.

Literary criticism was lagging hopelessly behind
events. Fiction was on the move, but slowly. But
poetry was mobile ... I chose the rostrum as my
battleground. I recited poetry in factories, colleges,
research institutes, in office buildings and schools. The
audiences numbered between twenty and a thousand.
In 1963 [poetry readings] attracted 14,000 people to
the Sports Palace.[4]

Where else could this have happened? Poetry was the
vehicle of political discourse. The inflections of the voice
were pregnant with meaning. One of the great Russian
masters, Osip Mandelstam, once retorted to his long-
suffering wife: 'Why do you complain? Poetry is
respected only in this country – people are killed for it'.
This was prophetic. Mandelstam was indeed killed for a
poem which lampooned Stalin.

Khrushchev's relationship with the writers and artists
was like a piece of barbed wire, smooth in parts but
lacerative in others. He lacked the culture and self-
confidence to make his own judgments and, hence, was
too influenced by ideological bureaucrats. In retirement
he confessed that he should have read the works which
caused such a furore himself instead of relying on quot-
ations, taken out of their context. Although he enjoyed
the theatre immensely – he went regularly in Moscow in
the 1930s and afterwards whenever he could – he was
unwilling to enter into a critical discussion of plays, especially of their artistic merit. Culture became a battleground. This was a tragedy since the intelligentsia were
strongly on his side in the war against Stalin's legacy.

Moscow welcomed many leaders from the Third World
after the congress: Kim Il-sung from North Korea,
Norodom Sihanouk from Cambodia, the Shah of Iran, and
Sukarno from Indonesia. All demonstrated the increasing
influence of the Soviet Union. Dag Hammerskjöld, the UN
secretary-general, also dropped in. The French prime

minister Guy Mollet also came, although Khrushchev observed that one did not pay much attention to the composition of French delegations since the government was always changing. This biting comment was true at the time but changed with the arrival of General de Gaulle and the Fifth Republic in 1958. A Soviet delegation, led by Mikoyan, went to Beijing in April 1956 and extended more economic aid to China. In his memoirs he scarcely conceals his contempt for China and the Chinese. Mao Zedong returned the compliment by visiting Moscow only once under Khrushchev. The experience put him off the Soviet capital for the rest of his life.

If Khrushchev knew deep down that relations with the Chinese could not blossom under Mao Zedong, Tito was quite a different proposition. Since the Soviets had come to him he could bargain hard and take revenge on his opponents in Eastern Europe. He demanded and got the dissolution of the Cominform, which had expelled Yugoslavia in 1948, and changes in the regimes which were most strongly anti-Titoist – Hungary, Romania and Bulgaria. The way was now clear for Tito's visit to the Soviet Union which took place in June 1956 and led to the resumption of links between the CPSU and the League of Communists of Yugoslavia. As a mark of respect to Tito, Khrushchev accompanied him around the USSR.

Denouncing Stalin and destroying the infallibility of the CPSU was like lighting a slow fuse under the East European communist regimes. Their legitimacy had been based on Stalin and the Soviet example. The first crisis came in Poland which had been quiescent when Czechoslovakia and the GDR had flared up after Stalin's death. Strikes and street fighting broke out in Poznan on 28 June. The Polish United Workers' Party sided with the workers, defused their anger and appeared to speak for Polish nationalism. Between July and September the Polish Party took decisions independently of Moscow and the leading light became Wladyslaw Gomulka, who had served time and been accused of being a Titoist or national communist. On 19 October the CC of the Polish Party convened to elect a new leader – Gomulka. What was Moscow to do? What were the implications of the Polish developments for socialism? Once they discovered the date of the CC meeting the Presidium decided to send Khrushchev, Mikoyan, Molotov and Kaganovich to Warsaw. It was unwilling to allow Nikita Sergeevich to go on his own. Such was the haste that no one informed the Poles and the Soviet aircraft when crossing the Polish frontier was intercepted by Polish fighters. This was an omen of what was to come. The Poles held their ground and refused to be browbeaten. Soviet troops were moved up to the Polish frontier. The Poles made it clear they would fight, led by the Party. They demanded and got the removal of Marshal Rokossovsky, their Soviet minister of defence. Poland promised to remain a close ally of the Soviet Union. The Soviet delegation returned home and left Poland to national communism.

The victory of Gomulka and the Poles appeared to signal that Moscow welcomed the elimination of Stalinism in Eastern Europe. This electrified the opposition in Hungary. The situation there was chaotic with the Party leadership disintegrating, the military losing control over its men and the security forces melting away. On 23 October 1956 a huge anti-regime demonstration in Budapest smashed the enormous Stalin statue and vented its spleen on everything Soviet and communist. The hated political police were a special target. Soviet forces tried to restore order but in vain. On 28 October Imre Nagy negotiated a ceasefire and the withdrawal of Soviet troops. The popular mood now was for an end to communist dictatorship and a return to democracy. On 1 November Nagy declared that Hungary had left the Warsaw Pact and was henceforth neutral. The Soviets, through their ambassador Yuri Andropov, misled the

Hungarian government about their true intentions. On 4 November they attacked and after bitter fighting took control of the country. Imre Nagy was arrested and later executed. János Kádár was installed as Party leader.

Hungary presented the divided Soviet leadership with agonizing choices. Khrushchev was blamed by some of his colleagues for the trouble because of his denunciation of Stalin. He was in the driving seat since Hungary was a socialist country. He needed the support of all socialist states if the intervention option were to be taken. The Chinese sent Liu Shao-chi. Intervention had to be agreed to by the other socialist states. Khrushchev and Malenkov flew off to consult with the leaders of Poland, Czechoslovakia, Romania and Bulgaria. They had no hesitation in favouring intervention. That left Yugoslavia. Malenkov and he then set off for Brioni Island to consult with Tito. It was a hazardous journey.

> We had to fly through the mountains at night in a fierce thunderstorm ... During the storm we lost contact with our escort reconnaissance plane which was flying ahead of us ... The local airfield was poorly equipped. It was one of those primitive airstrips built during the war ... There was a car waiting for us which took us to a pier. We climbed into a motor launch and headed for Comrade Tito's place on Brioni Island. Malenkov was as pale as a corpse. He gets car-sick on a good road ... He lay down in the boot and shut his eyes. I was worried about what kind of shape he'd be in when we docked, but we didn't have any choice.[5]

Khrushshev need not have worried. He did the talking. Tito went along with the decision to send the troops in and recommended speedy action. This sealed the Hungarians' fate. The Yugoslavs played a further role in the tragedy. Imre Nagy sought political asylum in the Yugoslav embassy in Budapest. A coach leaving the embassy was stopped and he was arrested. Who gave the order to snatch Nagy? Was it Khrushchev or was he faced with a *fait accompli*? When Nagy was executed two years later without a public trial Khrushchev was the master of the Soviet house. Surely he could have vetoed the execution if he had so desired. The whole episode soured relations with Yugoslavia.

Fortunately for the Soviet Union and unfortunately for Hungary a crisis had arisen in the Middle East at the same time. Britain, France and Israel attacked Egypt after President Nasser had nationalized the Suez Canal. The United States opposed the action and moreover had not been informed beforehand. The Soviet Union came out very strongly on Egypt's side and warned the belligerents that Soviet forces were ready to aid Egypt. The anti-Egyptian coalition backed off. The Soviets could claim some of the credit for the Egyptian victory and they had managed this without becoming involved. This whetted Nikita Sergeevich's appetite for a greater role in the Middle East. Britain and France were clearly declining powers there so why should the Soviet Union not play the guardian of Arab interests? Khrushchev rushed in where wiser counsels in the leadership would have feared to tread. Despite its military alliance with Egypt and the extension of substantial aid, such as the building of the Aswan high dam, Moscow, in the end, reaped few benefits. The Middle East safari would be held against him when he was being dismissed in 1964.

The failed putsch

The events of 1956 increased opposition to Khrushchev in the Presidium. He had provided enough hostages to fortune for his critics to argue that he was a liability. However, they were not united. Fortunately 1956 was a great agricultural success. Nikita Sergeevich was awarded the Order of Lenin and a second Hero of Socialist Labour award for his Virgin Land policies. However, the mess in Hungary had to be cleared up and the Soviets had to pay. This meant less investment elsewhere.

The decision to release millions from the gulag raised another unwelcome problem. Several whole nationalities had been branded as traitors and deported to the east in 1944. These people began returning and wanted their land and homes back from the settlers, mainly Russian and Ukrainian, who had occupied them. It was more simple in some cases than others. The Volga-German autonomous republic, dissolved in 1941, could not be restored. Neither could the Crimean Tatar region in the Crimea. Not even Gorbachev has found a solution yet to these two problems. All the nationalities were rehabilitated. The whole episode had been a ghastly mistake. When the Chechen-Ingush were given back their autonomous republic it was revealed that the NKVD had wiped out a whole village which had refused to move east. A commission was set up but the finger was pointed at Kruglov, the minister of internal affairs. Before it could report, he committed suicide.

A move which made Khrushchev unpopular with the upper echelons of the Party and state officials was the ending of supplementary payments. Sometimes they were three times the nominal salary.

Opposition within the Presidium was given a powerful boost by Khrushchev's proposal to abolish the ministries (except those in defence industries) concerned with the economy. The running of the economy was to be devolved to *sovnarkhozy* or councils of the national economy. Buoyed up by the excellent harvest of 1956 Nikita Sergeevich threw caution to the winds. He had a brainwave and claimed that the Soviet Union could catch up with the United States in per capita production of meat, milk and butter within three or four years. This might have been possible as regards milk and butter since US consumption was falling. However, meat was quite another story. Khrushchev thought, against all expert advice, that Soviet meat production could be trebled in five years. He also brushed aside all opposition in the Presidium. Here was clear evidence that Nikita Sergeevich had a utopian streak in him. He was so taken up with his numerous initiatives that he did not perceive that a coalition was forming against him in the Presidium.

Khrushchev's liking for foreign travel provided his enemies with time to plot against him. Bulganin and he left for Finland on 5 June, returning on 14 June 1957. Molotov, Malenkov and Kaganovich arranged for a meeting of the Presidium on 18 June to bring opposition to Khrushchev to a head and to remove him as first secretary. The new first secretary would be Vyacheslav Molotov. If Khrushchev agreed to go quietly he would be made minister of agriculture. If he resisted he could be arrested. This would have been difficult to implement since the military under Zhukov and the KGB under Serov were loyal to Khrushchev. Molotov and his co-conspirators were confident since they already knew they had a solid majority against him. All full and candidate members, except Frol Kozlov, were present. The guard around the Kremlin had been strengthened. The first secretary was accused of economic voluntarism – arbitrary and hasty policies. However, the main thrust against him was that he had gone too far in debunking Stalin and had thereby undermined the authority of the CPSU in the international communist movement and the movement itself. Khrushchev vigorously rejected the accusations and pointed to the economic and foreign policy achievements. He was strongly supported by only three members of the Presidium, Mikoyan, Suslov and Kirichenko. Seven Presidium members, including Molotov, Malenkov, Voroshilov, Kaganovich and Bulganin opposed him. Five candidate members, headed by Zhukov and Brezhnev, also sided with him but as candidate members they could speak but not vote. Brezhnev's speech was very crudely interrupted by Kaganovich. He was so shocked that he almost fainted. One intervention made quite an impact, that of Zhukov. Though only a candidate member he made quite clear that the military supported Khrushchev and would not move without his (Zhukov's) order. Shepilov began by supporting Khrushchev, then during the heated discussions changed sides. The Presidium passed a motion dismissing Khrushchev as first secretary. Backed up by his supporters Khrushchev refused to accept this decision. He argued that he had not been elected first secretary by the Presidium but by the CC. Only the CC could dismiss him. He demanded that a plenum of the CC be convened but the Presidium refused. Molotov and Malenkov had not taken into consideration the growth of the authority of the CC since 1953. They still thought that the country could be run by about twenty top politicians. When Kozlov, who was in Leningrad to celebrate the 250th anniversary of the founding of the city, heard about what was going on in Moscow he and other CC members immediately made for the capital. Zhukov and Serov made sure that almost all members of the CC got to Moscow quickly. The Presidium continued to refuse to convene a CC plenum and to meet CC representatives. When the Presidium majority were confident that they had won the day they sent Bulganin and Voroshilov to talk to CC members. However, Khrushchev and Mikoyan also went out with them. Voroshilov swore at Serov. The latter threatened that the CC would convene with or without the Presidium's permission since the issue was so vital. The Presidium had to give in because practically all CC members were in Moscow since the Presidium had been in permanent session for almost three days. The CC plenum lasted from 22–29 June and it was a foregone conclusion that Khrushchev would win. Molotov was the only comrade to oppose Nikita Sergeevich in the CC. The others backed down, changed sides and made penitential speeches.

Even Malenkov confessed his guilt. Molotov fought bitterly to the end even though his cause was hopeless. The CC resolution was passed with only Molotov abstaining.

The decree of the plenum and a short description of what had happened was only published on 4 July 1957. Mention was made of an 'Anti-Party group', consisting of Malenkov, Kaganovich, Molotov and Shepilov, 'who joined them'. The opposition of Bulganin, Voroshilov and the others was passed over in silence. The first two even kept their posts. Molotov, Malenkov, Kaganovich and Shepilov were dropped from the Presidium and the CC. One other lost his Presidium membership and another was demoted to candidate status. The Presidium was enlarged to fifteen members and among the new full members were Leonid Brezhnev, Frol Kozlov and Marshal Georgy Zhukov. Among the new candidate members were Aleksei Kosygin and Andrei Kirilenko. Molotov, Malenkov and Kaganovich were also dismissed from their posts as first deputy prime ministers. Andrei Gromyko replaced Shepilov as foreign minister. Although Ivan Serov, the head of the KGB, had also played an important part he was not promoted to membership of the Presidium. The head of the KGB would have to wait until the 1970s before it was judged opportune to elevate him to the supreme Party body.

At least one of the losers feared for his life. Two days after the plenum Khrushchev received a phone call from Kaganovich.

'Comrade Khrushchev, I have known you for many years. I beg you not to allow them to deal with me as they dealt with people under Stalin'.

He replied: 'Comrade Kaganovich, your words confirm once again what methods you wanted to use to attain your vile ends. You wanted the country to revert to the order that existed under the personality cult. You wanted to kill people. You measure others by your own yardstick. But you are mistaken. We apply Leninist principles with vigour and will continue to apply them. You will be given a job. You will be able to work and live in peace if you work honestly like all Soviet people.[6]

None of Khrushchev's adversaries were expelled at that time from the Party but was merely given a job far away from Moscow. Molotov was made ambassador to Mongolia. Kaganovich became director of a plant in the Urals. Malenkov was posted to Kazakhstan to look after a power plant. Shepilov was made a professor in Central Asia. In July 1957 two other losers ceased to be first deputy prime ministers and were replaced by Aleksei Kosygin and Dmitri Ustinov. Khrushchev and Bulganin left soon afterwards for a visit to Czechoslovakia. Nikita Sergeevich, in very frank conversations with the Yugoslav ambassador in Moscow, Micunovic, revealed that he did not care to travel with Bulganin but duties of state obliged him to do so. The ambassador had suggested to Khrushchev that it would not look good internationally if Bulganin was immediately dropped as prime minister. It was only a matter of time before Bulganin ceased going through the motions as prime minister. Voroshilov was allowed to stay on as head of state until 1960. Nikita Sergeevich could feel very pleased with himself. *De jure* he was head of the Party but *de facto* he was also prime minister and head of state.

It may seem strange to label Khrushchev's opponents the 'Anti-Party group'. After all they were members of the Presidium. The reason was that they, with their power bases in government, opposed the Party performing economic functions. The new Presidium revealed the shift in the balance of power between the government and the Party. Previously those holding government posts dominated; now those in Party jobs predominated.

The Party apparatus had taken over and was to retain its dominant position until Gorbachev became executive president in 1989.

With victory behind him Khrushchev took his first extended holiday for decades. He and his family enjoyed the Crimea near Yalta for almost a whole month. He must have felt very secure. If the success of Khrushchev at the June plenum had surprised the outside world something new in store would stun them.

On 4 October 1957, two days after Nikita Sergeevich got back from vacation, the Soviet Union amazed and stunned the world by launching the first artificial earth satellite, the Sputnik. So great was the surprise in the

Cartoon by Vicky published in the Daily Mirror *(December 1957) depicting great successes of Khrushchev: Sputnik; the firing of Zhukov; the Bulganin and Khrushchev double act (B&K); Tito and his balancing act between East and West; and Malenkov, who had been sent to run a power plant in the east.*

United States, for example, that many did not believe it. Vice-President Richard Nixon assured people that there really was nothing up there circling the earth! Sputnik revealed the great strides in Soviet missile technology and the potential to build intercontinental ballistic missiles (ICBM). A month later another satellite was launched, this time with a dog on board. The Americans began a feverish review of their missile technology but were not able to get a satellite into space until February 1958. Used to predominance for so long, the Americans now had a battle on their hands. They adjusted their technical education accordingly.

Sputnik was a marvellous present for the fortieth anniversary of the October Revolution which was celebrated with great *élan* on 7 November 1957. Almost all Communist Parties attended. This afforded Khrushchev the opportunity to redefine relationships in the wake of the debunking of Stalin. He was keen to see de-Stalinization set in motion in all parties. Two conferences were held: one of the twelve ruling parties and the other in which sixty-four communist and workers' parties participated. The speeches were not published; only a final declaration and a peace manifesto. Buoyed up by his great victory and the success of Sputnik and given his views on Mao Zedong and China, the scene was set for an epic encounter between the two communist Titans. With Stalin gone Mao saw himself as the doyen of the world communist movement. In Chinese culture age is always venerated. Shmuel Mikunis, then leader of the Israeli Communist Party, writing later, captures Mao's vanity nicely.

In the way he spoke and held himself, and in the way he replied to questions, he resembled a sage of ancient China ... He had trouble with his legs and usually spoke sitting down. His favourite theme, to which he kept returning, was World War III. He regarded this as an absolutely inevitable event ... I well remember how he sat there, surrounded by Soviet delegates, and philosophized aloud: 'Nehru and I,' he said 'are at present discussing the question of how many people would perish in an atomic war. Nehru says that we'll lose a billion and a half, but I say only a billion and a quarter.' Palmiro Togliatti then asked him: 'But what would become of Italy as a result of such a war?' Mao Zedong looked at him in a thoughtful way and replied quite coolly 'But who told you that Italy must survive? Three hundred million Chinese will survive, and that will be enough for the survival of the human race.' Mao saw himself as the leader of world communism, the direct successor of Stalin, and therefore assumed that he had the right to intervene in the affairs of all Communist Parties, including the Soviet Party. He talked a lot ... he did not so much talk as insist ... For instance, he was very displeased at Khrushchev's having removed Molotov, Malenkov and Kaganovich from the leadership and said: 'You should have consulted me before you took that step.'[7]

As the natural successor to Stalin Mao felt he should have a say in Soviet developments. He was on a collision course with Khrushchev from the beginning. Another matter of great importance on which they could not agree was nuclear weapons. He had even greater faith in them than Nikita Sergeevich. However, he argued that if the Soviet Union had nuclear superiority it should use its power to destroy the American 'imperialists'. To Mao the Americans were 'paper tigers' but to Khrushchev they were real tigers. The latter had a much greater grasp of the responsibilities resting upon nuclear powers than the Chinese leader. Also, China possessed no nuclear capability at this time.

Marshal Georgy Zhukov had proved himself an innovative minister of defence. He set off for a tour of Yugoslavia and Albania in early October but while he was in the latter country he was dismissed. A CC plenum had been called and he went straight from the airport to the Kremlin. In the summer of 1957 he had introduced some military reforms without first consulting the Party. One of them obliged political officers to study military theory alongside professional officers. He treated the political officers with contempt and wished to evolve a purely professional army. This was a direct threat to Party control over the armed forces. He was sacked from the Presidium and the CC and transferred to 'other work', which never materialized. Embittered, he set about writing his memoirs, which were later to cause Khrushchev almost to choke in annoyance. The new minister of defence was Marshal Rodion Malinovsky, whom Khrushchev great annoyance. The new minister of defence was Marshal Rodion Malinovsky, whom Khrushchev knew well from his days on the Ukrainian front. He made sure he picked a man who was pliable. Khrushchev had in mind military reforms in the wake of Sputnik. Zhukov would have regarded Khrushchev, a mere civilian, as unqualified to introduce military reform. So Nikita Sergeevich parted company with a man who had played a vital role in the defeat of Beria and the 'Anti-Party group'. He would brook no opposition in his crusade to make the Party supreme.

On Top of the World, 1958-62

4

The New Year's Eve reception in the Kremlin was a glittering occasion. It was attended by the high and mighty, great and good. They all sang Khrushchev's praises. When, in March 1958, Bulganin was pushed aside and he assumed the functions of prime minister he was, in retrospect, at the zenith of his power. He had become a strong national leader. A Defence Council was established to coordinate military policy and naturally Nikita Sergeevich became commander-in-chief of Soviet armed forces. All the glittering prizes offered by the Party and state were his. It was enough to turn anyone's head.

He had accumulated great power but what about authority? The latter is absolutely vital if policies are to be effectively implemented. Authority is conferred on a leader voluntarily by the population. His authority in the Party apparatus was very high. After all many owed their promotion to him and quite a few careers were just beginning to take off. How would he use his power? If he merely wished to rule like a potentate all he had to do was to concentrate on eliminating challenges to his position. However, if he wished to transform the country he would have to build tactical coalitions and convince the population that his measures would benefit them.

It quickly transpired that Nikita Sergeevich had no intention of resting on his laurels. Power was to be deployed to erase the Stalinist legacy. Leninist tradition now became the guiding beacon. However, he interpreted Lenin through the distorting glass of the Stalin era. He had not mastered the Marxist classics either so he was ill prepared to engage in ideological innovation. He would now need to develop other talents. He had proved himself a brilliant political infighter, capable time and again of surprising his opponents and the world. Khrushchev now needed the ability to analyse carefully a problem, examine several possible solutions, select the most apposite solution and then introduce it when the time was right. New legislations would involve public debate since the Party and state apparatus and the public at large had to support it if it were to be successfully implemented.

Khrushchev had great political gifts but he needed a team to tackle the economic and other problems bequeathed by the Stalin era. Ideally he needed a talented supporter who had extensive experience of industry and agriculture and who could coordinate and implement economic policy. Someone like Malenkov would have fitted the bill. He could have been made prime minister. However, Khrushchev became head of the Party and the government and this made it very difficult for a colleague to play a leading role. A man was waiting in the wings, one who could have contributed greatly to improving economic performance: Aleksei Kosygin. He was a first deputy prime minister and candidate member of the Presidium. However, he was more concerned with technical matters than political infighting. It was a tragedy that Nikita Sergeevich did not make more use of Kosygin's talents. Apparently he did propose him as prime minister in 1958 but the general consensus in the Presidium was that Khrushchev should occupy both posts. Kosygin might have had a restraining influence on Nikita Sergeevich's brilliant but erratic ideas. He was at his reforming peak between 1958 and 1962 – he could force through any piece of legislation – but it must be admitted that much of it was ill conceived, ill digested and doomed to fail before the ink was dry on the documents. There was no overall plan, no strategy of reform. It usually began with Nikita Sergeevich having a wizard idea. So enthusiastic would he become that he would brush aside all objections. He was brilliant at lateral thinking – providing several solutions to the same problem. As time passed the number of options declined and he often chose the wrong one. He would dictate his inspirational thoughts, then read the transcript, make amendments and finally hand it over for drafting as legislation. There were formidabie institutional barriers to radical change in the Soviet Union – Gorbachev has demonstrated this time and time again – but it is clear that the personal factor also played an important role. Khrushchev believed passionately that he had a mission – to transform the Soviet Union into a land of plenty in which justice and democracy would reign. As an evangelist he was as full of eloquence as he was empty of doubt about the communist goal. Unfortunately the number of doubters increased steadily so that by 1964 there were practically no believers left. Nikita Sergeevich personally must shoulder much of the blame for this débâcle.

His great enthusiasm during the summer and autumn of 1958 was education. He was shocked to discover during a lecture at Moscow University that the great majority of students were from the intelligentsia. One factor which favoured this was the need to pay fees for college tuition and the upper forms of secondary school – legislation introduced by Stalin. Only the very gifted could break through – one of these was Gorbachev but he was there due mainly to Party patronage. Nikita Sergeevich was a man of the soil and believed in the ennobling effect of physical labour. Too many in the intelligentsia looked upon manual labour with disdain – it was something to escape from. Polytechnical education was seen as the solution with secondary school pupils engaging in practical work several hours a week. Local factories could introduce them to the world of work. Primary schooling was to be extended from seven to eight years. After leaving school students were to work in the economy for at least two years and then move on to higher education. They would be prepared for this by day-release and night-school instruction. Payment for tuition was abolished. Typically Khrushchev's proposals were not based on detailed research into the existing system but on his own experiences. The legislation was passed in December 1958 and school reform was to be completed over a five-year period. At the last moment it was decided to reduce the overall period of schooling from eleven to ten years. This made life even more difficult for schools and teachers. The intelligentsia, on the whole, did not like the reform. They did not want their children to tend a lathe or pick potatoes. Exceptions were permitted. A very gifted musician or mathematician would be of more value to the state if allowed to concentrate on academic studies. The point was made that a very talented young pianist would cease to be one if he lost a finger in a machine. Since universities controlled entry they could always ensure that the 'right' students were admitted. Hence in the end the reform ran into the sand.

The time had also come to reform the KGB. It was full of officers, beginning with Ivan Serov, the head, whose pasts were murky, to put it mildly. Roy Medvedev thinks that the scandal of the Queen of the Belgians' crown provided an ideal pretext. The crown had been looted by the Germans during the war and had disappeared. After a long investigation it turned out to be in Serov's very extensive personal collection. He was as avid a magpie as

Marshal Hermann Göring. Serov had bagged it while working for *Smersh* (Soviet counter-intelligence) in Germany. The crown was returned. Serov was too useful to Khrushchev to be disgraced. He was made head of the GRU or military intelligence and its activities were beyond public scrutiny.

Khrushchev nominated Aleksandr Shelepin, first secretary of the Komsomol or Young Communist League, as the new head. Shelepin was young, dynamic and ferociously ambitious. He turned the KGB upside down and brought in a large number of Komsomol officials. This promised to make the security police a Party tool. However, Khrushchev misjudged Shelepin and was later to fall victim to his plotting.

Talented figures in the literary world were impatient to publish what they had been writing in private. It was kept in the 'bottom drawer', as the expression goes. V. Dudintsev published *Not by Bread Alone* in 1956. The novel is about a scientist who has to fight the establishment – scholars, managers and Party officials. The journal *Novy Mir*, under its chief editors Konstantin Simonov and Aleksandr Tvardovsky, became one of the focal points of the new era. Boris Pasternak offered his 'bottom drawer' novel *Dr Zhivago* to *Novy Mir* but was turned down. It favoured democratic socialism and thus was not willing to give a platform to Pasternak's rejection of the October Revolution. The work ended up in the hands of a left-wing Italian publisher, Feltrinelli. He published it in 1957 and the following year Pasternak was awarded the Nobel Prize. The establishment descended on Pasternak like a pack of wolves. *Literaturnaya Gazeta* referred to him as 'a literary Judas who has betrayed his people for thirty pieces of silver, the Nobel Prize'. Vladimir Semichastny, first secretary of the Komsomol, was more down to earth. He called the author a 'pig who had fouled his own sty'. One doctor claimed that the novel was a disgrace to the medical profession. A terrible joke circulated: 'Moscow is suffering from three plagues: *rak* (cancer), Spartak, (a Moscow football team doing badly) and Pasternak.' He declined the Nobel Prize. The episode shortened his life and when he died in May 1960 his funeral brought together a latent independent intelligentsia. Their presence was a protest against the oppressive nature of the regime. The whole disgraceful episode lost the Soviet Union face abroad. In retirement, after having read the novel, Khrushchev regretted his actions. Party cultural bureaucrats had misled him by quoting selected passages, out of context.

Another group with which Khrushchev was frequently at loggerheads was the military. The defence budget was cut in 1953 and 1954 and Khrushchev was hungry for more. By 1958 the military had lost two million men. Khrushchev began to see missiles as the weapons of the future. He had clashed with Zhukov, a solidly ground forces' man, over this. In December 1959 the Strategic Rocket Forces were established as a separate service responsible for regional and intercontinental missile forces. These forces were declared to be the pre-eminent forces in wartime, replacing the ground forces. In a speech to the Supreme Soviet in January 1960 Khrushchev declared the primary importance of nuclear weapons and missiles. He emphasized that many of the traditional armed forces were becoming obsolete. Manpower was to drop from 3.6 million to 2.4 million. Nuclear firepower would more than make up for the cut in manpower.

How large was the Soviet nuclear arsenal? In late 1959 Khrushchev and Marshal Malinovsky made statements which implied that the Soviets were pressing ahead with an ICBM building programme and they claimed nuclear parity with the US. In early 1960 Khrushchev claimed the capability to wipe off the map any country which dared to attack the Soviet Union, by using rockets carrying atomic and thermonuclear warheads. In reality this capacity did not exist. By 1960 the USSR had deployed a total of 4 ICBMs and 145 heavy bombers of inter-continental range. Khrushchev's boasting backfired. The Americans began to perceive a 'missile gap' and set about eliminating it.

The reasons behind Khrushchev's high risk strategy appear to be his exaggerated belief in missiles, the loom-ing labour shortage due to the drastic fall in the birth rate during the war and the need to save money. Nuclear forces are cheaper than conventional forces the world over. Khrushchev was changing Soviet military doctrine but many top officers disagreed with his premises. There were other grievances. No preparations had been made to ease the transition of the demobbed officers and men into civilian life.

He then turned his attention to the police. He proposed abolishing the all-union Ministry of Internal Affairs and devolving their duties to republican Ministries for the Safeguarding of Public Order (MOOP). The civil police, the militia and the MOOP officers were to lose some of their material privileges. These, according to Khrushchev, had become excessive under Stalin. Nikita Sergeevich was making himself unpopular with the guard-ians of national and domestic security. Neither did he enamour himself to those working in Siberia and the Soviet Far East. After visiting the regions he decided that the many bonuses and benefits paid to workers there should be abolished. This accelerated migration from the east to the more hospitable regions of European Russia and the south. This policy had later to be reversed in order to attract labour to the new industries, especially oil and natural gas.

There was a leadership reshuffle in May 1960. A CC plenum promoted Aleksei Kosygin, Nikolai Podgorny and Dmitri Polyansky to full membership of the Presidium. Those going down included Andrei Kirichenko who was dismissed from the Presidium and the Secretariat. He had been a close Khrushchev ally and had chaired meetings of the Presidium and Secretariat when Nikita Sergeevich was away on one of his jaunts. He may have been blamed for the agricultural failures of 1959. He was replaced as a CC secretary by Frol Kozlov. The latter had his detractors in Leningrad where he worked but Khrushchev ignored these rumblings. Another comrade to go from the Presidium was Nikolai Belyaev, first Party secretary in Kazakhstan. He had promised more than he delivered in the prime Virgin Lands region. His successor was the Kazakh Dinmukhamed Kunaev. Voroshilov was at long last removed as head of state and replaced by Leonid Brezhnev.

One measure which pleased many was the abolition of income tax and the tax on bachelors and spinsters earning less than 500 rubles a month. A seven-hour working day was gradually to be introduced. Another monetary reform was not welcomed. As of 1 January 1961 ten old rubles were to be worth one new ruble. People simply did not believe the ruble in their pocket had retained its value. Psychologically a large amount of notes seems to confer a nice warm feeling. This is one of the reasons why Italians earn millions of lire a month. The suspicions of the Soviet population were well founded. State prices stayed firm but the private market saw the change as a heaven-sent opportunity to make some extra money.

Foreign policy

Khrushchev's courtship of Tito did not lead to warmer relations Indeed the Yugoslav communists went their own way and a draft programme published in the summer of 1958 was judged 'revisionist' by Soviet ideologues. This was a very insulting term and raised the hackles of Belgrade. Khrushchev went further and referred to Yugoslavia as a Trojan horse in the world communist movement. He also postponed the granting of credits which were to begin in 1958 and stopped the shipment of wheat which had already been agreed. In both cases he broke contractual agreements but that was Nikita Sergeevich's style.

Relations with China became more difficult in 1958. The Chinese regarded a third world war as inevitable but Khrushchev did not. They also took Nikita Sergeevich's boasting about Soviet missile advances far too seriously. As a result they thought he was being too soft on the capitalist world. Mao's 'Great Leap Forward' to communism was underway and more and more demands were being made for Soviet and East European help. China began to browbeat Taiwan by shelling some offshore islands. The Americans sent in their fleet and Beijing expected Moscow to see them off. When Khrushchev visited the Chinese capital he merely stated that in the event of a serious conflict the Soviet Union would be on China's side. The Chinese felt let down. He was also asked to help China develop its own nuclear capacity. Mao understood Khrushchev as committing himself to this policy but Moscow has always denied this.

Opportunities arose to play a more influential role in the Middle East in the summer of 1958. The pro-British regime in Iraq was overthrown and Jordan felt threatened. So too did Lebanon. So American troops were invited into Lebanon. The Arabs sought Soviet support. Furious diplomatic exchanges ensued between Moscow and Washington. Nasser travelled to the Soviet capital and lobbied for Soviet troops. The Americans withdrew their troops from Lebanon. It was quite a diplomatic victory for Khrushchev.

Nikita Sergeevich's delight in foreign travel took him often to Eastern Europe where he played the lord of the manor. In May 1959 he went to Albania and did not get on at all with the leadership. It was Stalinist and was quite determined to stay Stalinist. Enver Hoxha, the Party leader, felt threatened by domestic pressure for reform and the attempts of Moscow and Belgrade to normalize relations. Some members of the Party opposition travelled to Moscow to lobby Khrushchev's support. Three top Albanian Party officials were shot on Hoxha's orders. Appeals by Khrushchev for leniency fell on deaf ears. One of those shot was a pregnant woman. Khrushchev also records that an Albanian leader, another woman, en route from Beijing to Tirana, on the stopover in Moscow, briefed the Soviets on what had been discussed. She was strangled for this indiscretion. It came as no surprise when Albania broke with the Soviet Union in 1961. It also left the Warsaw Pact and Comecon, the socialist trade organization. The Albanians became fierce critics of the Soviet Union and Nikita Sergeevich was a special target for their venom.

Visiting the GDR in March 1959 he was encouraged by Walter Ulbricht, the Party leader, to find a solution to the Berlin problem. Ulbricht explained that socialism could not be built in the GDR as long as the open frontier in Berlin remained. By 1961 over three million East Germans would have moved to the West. Berlin was a very sensitive issue. East met West there militarily face to face. To Khrushchev the city was a barometer. The 'slightest fluctuation in the pressure of the world political atmosphere naturally registered at the point where the forces of the two sides squared up to one another'. The only option left to Moscow, since reunification was out of the question, was a treaty confirming the existence of two German states. East Berlin was run by the East Germans and West Berlin was closely linked to West Germany. Soviet and East German policy was to prise the West out of West Berlin. Berlin would then become the capital of socialist Germany and would be a magnet to West Germans. The Berlin crisis began in November 1958 and lasted about four years. Khrushchev launched it by stating that the situation was abnormal and that the status quo was unacceptable. West Berlin should be transformed into a 'free city' with the Western allies quitting the city. It was an ultimatum. Should the West not agree by May 1959 a treaty would be signed with the GDR handing over Soviet rights to them. The West would have to negotiate access to West Berlin with the GDR, which as a member of the Warsaw Pact could call on the aid of that organization if disputes arose. A unification treaty could be negotiated by the two German states but Germany would be neutral. Communists would be given a free hand politically but 'revanchist and revisionist' groups would be banned.

The West rejected the ultimatum but proposed the examination of the German question in the wider context of European security. A foreign ministers' conference was convened in Geneva in May and Moscow lifted its ultimatum. It got nowhere but the Western goal was to keep the Soviets talking lest Khrushchev do something rash.

The Berlin crisis forced the Americans and the Soviets to talk to one another. Anastas Mikoyan flew to the US and met President Eisenhower and Secretary of State John Foster Dulles and discussed a wide range of issues.

In June 1959 the eagerly awaited American exhibition opened in Sokolniki Park in Moscow. Vice-President Richard Nixon was there to wave the flag. He showed Khrushchev around with each politician trying to score points off the other. They ended up in the kitchen of the model American home and Khrushchev was feeling the strain. There then followed one of the most famous exchanges in US–Soviet relations. Irritated by the effortless superiority of his host, Nikita Sergeevich delivered himself of an earthy saying. His message was that if the Americans wanted to have a go, the Soviets would teach them a lesson. However, the US interpreter was flummoxed by the expression and translated it literally: 'We'll show you Kuzma's mother'. This gave rise to great hilarity afterwards with the expression being used as a euphemism for a sensitive part of the male anatomy.

Khrushchev got his invitation to America. It was revealed in July 1959 that he was to pay an official visit between 15 and 28 September to 'get to know the country and the people'. President Eisenhower was to return the visit later. The visit would be the first by the head of the Soviet government or Party. His entourage included Nina Petrovna, his wife, and other members of his family, Andrei Gromyko and his wife, Sholokhov, the writer, and Nikolai Tikhonov, later to become prime minister. Khrushchev was very excited about the visit.

Who would have guessed, twenty years ago, that the most powerful capitalist country would invite a communist to visit? This is incredible. Today they *have* to take us into account. It's our strength that led to this – they have to recognize our existence and our power. Who would have thought the capitalists would invite me, a worker? Look what we've achieved in these years.[1]

Uncle Sam loved Nikita Sergeevich. His dynamism, openness, earthiness, love of good drink, vitality and sheer *joie de vivre* went down a treat. An American look-alike made a good living afterwards by impersonating Nikita Sergeevich.

He gave as good as he got. Challenged by the Washington press on human rights and other sensitive issues he exclaimed: 'If you throw dead rats at me, I'll throw dead rats at you!' In Washington he met John F. Kennedy for the first time. In New York he addressed the UN and stressed the need for peaceful coexistence, disarmament and avoidance of nuclear war – common themes throughout his US visit. In Los Angeles he was riled by the mayor's speech which was sharp and wounding. Nikita Sergeevich then performed his exploding act. He made it clear he represented a great power and would not be treated thus. He asked if his plane was ready. It

was not far to Vladivostok. Later the lugubrious Andrei
Gromyko was despatched to convey the same message
to Henry Cabot Lodge who was accompanying the Soviet
delegation around the country. The next day, in San
Francisco, all was sweetness and light. Not a hint of
criticism was to be heard. Nikita Sergeevich's act had
worked. Walter Reuther and other trade union leaders
did not let Khrushchev off so lightly. Their discussions
were animated, to say the least. He also visited Iowa and
indulged in his passion for maize. The last part of the trip
was devoted to talks with President Eisenhower and the
expression 'the Camp David spirit' was coined after their
meeting place. He had already had discussions with
Eisenhower after his arrival. The two got on well but
nothing substantial came of the discussions. The Soviet
Union would not submit to international inspection to
ensure that disarmament agreements were being
observed. On Germany Eisenhower offered a summit and
Khrushchev lifted his ultimatum. Khrushchev later said
that his visit had broken the ice; it was now up to the
diplomats to remove the lumps. He picked up a few
useful tips as well. Self-service restaurants were a revela-
tion and were adopted in the Soviet Union. Then he
discovered that many Americans travelled by train at
night in sleeping compartments. That too was taken on
board at home in a big way. The US visit was given enormous publicity in the Soviet Union and left a lasting
impression.

Khrushchev set off for Beijing the day after he arrived
back from the US. However, his promotion of détente with
the Americans was the last straw for Mao Zedong.
Hobnobbing with the 'imperialists' was something a
Soviet leader should not be doing, in the eyes of the
Chinese. His contact with Mao was short. The Chinese
sage explained that he was too busy. This underlined the
fact that the Soviets and Chinese had little to say to one
another. Increasing friction was developing between

Soviet and East European advisers and their Chinese hosts, bent as they were in implementing the 'Great Leap Forward'. It caused economic damage and the advisers were right in regarding it as the 'Great Leap Backward'. Khrushchev left quickly, soon to be followed by the advisers. One point particularly riled the Chinese: they took the blueprints with them. This strengthened autarkic tendencies in China and they vowed never to become dependent on an outside power again. Sino-Soviet relations only returned to an even keel under Gorbachev. The rift was probably inevitable but it was hastened and deepened by Khrushchev's undiplomatic and insensitive behaviour. Courtesy, good manners and the avoidance of loss of face are very important to the Chinese.

In early 1960 he paid another visit to India, talked to Nehru and toured several cities and inspected the Bhilai steel works which was being built in collaboration with the Soviet Union. He moved on to Burma and finally to Indonesia. Various agreements on economic and cultural cooperation were signed. Students from the region were invited to study in the USSR. The latter were not popular since they were given preferential treatment. Homeward bound he dropped in on the Afghans.

Shortly after his return he was off again, to France. The country had a strong Communist Party but also powerful forces on the right. President de Gaulle was attempting to consolidate the young Fifth Republic. There were numerous clashes between left and right. Nikita Sergeevich toured the country and was introduced to vintage champagne. Being a wine he underestimated its potency. He ended up doing the *gopak*, a traditional dance. This involves a lot of jumping and bending and is best left to the young. Later he was to ask de Gaulle whether his foreign minister would do anything he asked. The response was positive. Whereupon Nikita Sergeevich expressed the view that Andrei Andreevich Gromyko would do anything for him. If ordered to drop his trousers and sit on a block of ice he would do so.

It was finally agreed that the summit meeting would take place in Paris on 16 May 1960. However, it was doomed before it started. An American reconnaissance plane was shot down by a Soviet anti-aircraft rocket over Sverdlovsk in the Urals on 1 May 1960. When Khrushchev reported this he did not give the location. The pilot, Gary Powers, was under orders to destroy his aircraft and not to provide any information. The Americans stated that an aircraft had been investigating meteorological conditions over Turkey and Iran and had strayed into Soviet airspace. Khrushchev then revealed the location and said that the aircraft had not been destroyed. Material on board showed that it had been photographing Soviet installations and the pilot had cooperated. The Soviet protest was not even acknowledged by the Americans.

In Paris Khrushchev demanded that Eisenhower condemn and cease all such overflights, punish those involved and apologize. The American president refused. His invitation to visit the Soviet Union was withdrawn. The two countries reverted to hurling abuse at one another.

The revolution in Cuba in 1959, led by Fidel Castro, became increasingly anti-American. This made a rapprochement with Moscow a natural development. The US imposed a trade embargo and left Castro no option but to deepen relations with the socialist world in order to survive. Khrushchev decided to attend the General Assembly of the UN in September 1960. This was very unwelcome news to the Americans who were in the throes of an election campaign between Richard Nixon and John F. Kennedy. Khrushchev decided to sail to America in the *Baltica* and invite along the Party leaders of Hungary, Romania and Bulgaria for the ride. The fact that the Soviet leader was going forced a whole host of world leaders to go as well. The *Baltica* docked not at one of the grand piers but at a miserable, dilapidated one. The reason for this apparently was that the Soviets were short of hard cash and wanted to spend as little money as possible. Hence they ended up among the poor relations. Khrushchev visited the Cuban delegation's modest hotel in Harlem for his first meeting with Castro. He also met Tito again. His speech was accorded star billing by the world media. Otherwise his behaviour was deliberately disruptive. He interrupted speakers from the floor (the Philippines delegate was disparagingly dismissed as a 'lackey of American imperialism'), he rowed with Dag Hammerskjöld over UN behaviour in the Congo, he proposed that a 'troika' replace the 'hopelessly biased' secretary-general and he banged his shoe on his desk to emphasize his displeasure. (Harold Macmillan, the British prime minister, responded by calmly asking for a translation!) Careful examination of this incident revealed that he was wearing two shoes at the time. It was all a bit of showmanship. The UN was not pleased and fined the Soviet delegation $10,000 for its bad behaviour. Embarrassed Soviet diplomats attempted to present 'shoe' diplomacy as something novel – which it certainly was – and which underlined Khrushchev's determination to fight imperialism. It was nothing of the kind and presented the Soviet leader in a very poor light. Such undisciplined behaviour suggested that the man in control in the Kremlin was not in control of himself. However, it may all have been pre-planned by Nikita Sergeevich. With the Soviet Union needing to cut defence expenditure, switch resources to the civil economy and overcome the shortage of labour caused by the drop in the birth rate during the war, he may have thought that the best way to scare off the Americans was to threaten them with his non-existent missile fleet. His unpredictable behaviour would warn the West that it was far too risky to put pressure on him. If this was his thinking then he miscalculated. Instead of slowing down the arms race he accelerated it. Better to assume he had all the missiles he claimed. Then he got carried away at times. He loved acting and putting on a show of anger. He had honed these skills in the Soviet Union but the outside world was different.

Increasing Chinese anger at the policies of the Soviet Union was not mere acting but the real thing. The gap between the Chinese, Yugoslav and Albanian Parties and the CPSU, despite all Khrushchev's efforts, was widening. Border clashes between China and India, in early 1960, added fuel to the fire. The frontier had been mapped out by the British colonial regime and was not very precise. The Chinese took it for granted that the Soviets would side with them. However, Moscow was cultivating India and merely published both the Chinese and Indian versions of the incident. A Soviet delegation, headed by Voroshilov, at the invitation of New Delhi, went to India in search of a solution. Soviet invitations to the Chinese government and Mao Zedong to visit Moscow went unanswered. The two communist giants were no longer on speaking terms. From now on it would be polemics instead. On the 90th anniversary of Lenin's birth, in April 1960, the Chinese published a lengthy analysis of Leninism and claimed that they, rather than the Soviets, were the true standard bearers of Leninist revolutionary tradition. Soviet and East European specialists left. The first head-on confront-ation in public took place during the Romanian Commun-ist Party Congress in June 1960. Khrushchev and the Chinese delegate fought for supremacy in front of embar-rassed delegates. It was agreed to convene another inter-national conference of Communist and Workers' Parties in Moscow in November 1960. Eighty-one parties were there but the Yugoslavs were not. It was a significant occasion. The CPSU was no longer accepted auto-matically as the leading Party and came in for hefty critic-ism on its home ground. Almost a dozen Parties supported the Chinese position. One can date the schism in the world communist movement from this date. Henceforth the Soviets and the Chinese would vie for supremacy. There were now two camps, with the Yugoslavs outside both. Under Lenin and Stalin communism was monocentric – Moscow rule prevailed – but it had now become polycentric. There were many roads to communism. The spell of the unified movement was still so strong that the Chinese, though outvoted, signed the final statement. However, this facade quickly disintegrated and the conference proved to be the last of its kind. Khrushchev's determination to pursue de-Stalinization had split the Soviet Union. Now it had split the world communist movement.

The Twenty-first Party Congress

With the Chinese sharply critical of his economic policies Nikita Sergeevich had to demonstrate that his innovations were brilliantly successful. However, the harvest did not come up to expectations in 1957 – the tradition under Khrushchev was that even years were good and odd years bad. He needed more consistency. It became clear that the Five-Year Plan 1956–60 would not attain its targets. Nikita Sergeevich had a brainwave. If five years were not enough to succeed why not introduce a seven-year plan? The best forum to launch such a plan was a Party congress. However, one was not due until 1960. Undaunted, Khrushchev called an extraordinary congress, the Twenty-first, in January 1959. Another advantage of an extraordinary congress is that reports of the period since the previous congress do not have to be delivered. Hence the embarrassing row with the Chinese could be put aside as well as explanations for the events surrounding the June 1957 plenum. The congress launched a very ambitious economic plan with industrial output to rise by 80 per cent by 1965. There was to be a chemical revolution; production was to rise by 300 per cent. Emphasis was to be concentrated on modern technologies, especially those pioneered by successes in space. Living standards were to rise sharply with many more consumer goods becoming available. Fifteen million flats were to be constructed and another seven million dwellings in the countryside.

Despite the euphoria engendered by these targets there were some bad omens. The decision to disband the Machine Tractor Stations was taken in an effort to make farms more self-reliant. Most farms, however, did not have the resources to buy the machinery and employ the repair staff necessary. Then the relentless pressure to boost agricultural production began to have undesirable side effects. Ryazan *oblast* promised to increase vastly meat deliveries to the state in 1959. How could this astonishing target be achieved? One way would be to decimate animal numbers but meat production would drop catastrophically in 1960 and thereafter. Someone came up with a better idea. Buy from the peasants. But this would only cover a proportion of what was needed. There were animals in other *oblasts* so why not rustle them? This could only be done at night so nocturnal expeditions took off in all directions to steal every animal that could be found. Rustling animals meant that the other *oblasts'* plans could not be fulfilled. However, that was their problem. To make up the deficit another wheeze was thought up. Buy animals from the peasants, record them as state deliveries, sell them back to the peasants, buy them back, sell them back, until the plan had been fulfilled – at least on paper! Sooner or later the balloon was bound to go up. When it did the first Party secretary went the way of his animals. He shot himself. Khrushchev was later to rail against the padding of production statistics but he should have known better. The penalty for failure was so high that 'success' had to be reported.

One of the reasons for the disappointing agricultural

performance was under-investment. There was a sharp reduction in investment in 1958 with the drop in the rate of growth of investment in agriculture falling from 12.8 per cent in 1958 to 7 per cent in 1959 to 2.4 per cent in 1960. During 1958–64 annual deliveries of trucks, grain combines, cultivators, seeders and maize silage harvesters dropped below the levels of 1956–57. The result was that the share of agriculture in total investment fell from 17.6 per cent in 1956 to 14.2 per cent in 1960 but rose to 17.4 per cent in 1964. Denied more resources for agriculture Nikita Sergeevich tried to compensate by launching campaigns to change cropping patterns. In this way he hoped that production would be boosted. He campaigned for the expansion of maize as a fodder crop and it replaced more suitable crops in many areas. Between 1953 and 1963 the area under rye was cut back by a quarter and under oats by just under two-thirds. Maize replaced winter wheat in the Ukraine and north Caucasus. However, lack of suitable machinery caused delays and resulted in poor crops and yields.

Needing to get more land under the plough Nikita Sergeevich's eyes fell on the area under grass and fallow. He relentlessly toured the country preaching against the prevailing practices. Again he was successful. Between 1960 and 1963 the area under grass was reduced by a half and under clean fallow by almost two-thirds. Leading agronomists, especially A. Baraev as a result of his experience in north Kazakhstan, opposed the reduction of fallow in dry farming zones. Khrushchev very rudely brushed his objections aside and advised that someone should put a flea up his shirt to wake him up. T.D. Lysenko, who dominated agronomy between 1948 and 1966, favoured early sowing of crops in the Virgin Lands to ensure that they ripened in time. Opponents warned of the dangers of soil erosion and weeds and argued for late sowing. This, combined with the policy of cutting back on fallow, resulted in weed infestation so great that grain was choked. Neither weedkillers nor machinery to till the land more often were available. In 1963 an early spring thaw and drought caused the soil to dry out in the Virgin Lands. The harvest failure was almost total and millions of tonnes of top-soil were blown away.

Khrushchev was aware that the various campaigns were no substitute for greater investment. After the disappointments of 1960 he called for more investment and had limited faith in campaigns to raise peasants' enthusiasm for their work. However, a powerful lobby opposed to diverting extra resources to the rural economy blocked him. Defence and heavy industry, at a time of increasing international tension, were accorded their usual priority.

Despite the damage done to the environment and the lack of extra cash, agricultural output continued to rise. Grain and animal husbandry output over the years 1961–64 were significantly higher than in 1957–60. Output, however, fell far short of expectations. By 1965 the actual increase was only 20 per cent of the planned increase set in 1958. This was all very disappointing from the consumers' point of view as they sought to improve their inadequate diets. Others were disillusioned as well. It occurred to Nikita Sergeevich that peasants were devoting too much time and energy to their private plots. He 'encouraged' them to sell their livestock to the socialist sector. They became less self-sufficient and turned to state shops to make up the shortfall. This increased the pressure on the state retail network. It also swelled migration from the country to the town. Peasant apathy and lack of control over what they did on the farms were crucial problems which had to be tackled if agriculture was to bloom.

The ministry of agriculture was held mainly responsible for the failures of 1960. It was downgraded to a research and advisory service with the State Planning

Commission (Gosplan) taking over the state farms and the Central Statistical Administration collecting production data and statistics. A new State Committee for Agricultural Procurement, operating through *oblast* Procurement Inspectorates, appeared to calculate production quotas and supervise their attainment on collective farms. Farm management became the responsibility of many agencies and as the deliniation of duties was imprecise, conflicts inevitably arose. This was one reason why the reform did not have the desired effect.

In March 1962 Khrushchev proposed a revamping of agricultural administration. The State Committee for Agricultural Procurement was dissolved and a new unified administrative structure was established, headed by an All-Union Committee for Agriculture and supervised by a hierarchy of Party-dominated agricultural committees. The basic units were almost one thousand Territorial Production Associations (TPAs). Each TPA was assigned a Party organizer and he was responsible for about sixty farms. He was the agent of the obkom to ensure that farms fulfilled their plans. (Gorbachev became a Party organizer in Stavropol *krai.*) The official appointed to chair the All-Union Committee, N.G. Ignatov, demoted from the Party Presidium, was later to play an important role in coordinating opposition to Khrushchev in 1964. He was typical of many others who felt let down by Khrushchev.

In November 1962 the whole Party and local soviet apparatus was reorganized along production lines. Each *oblast* and *raion* committee was divided into separate committees for industry and agriculture. At the lowest level, the *raion* gave way to 'zones of industrial production' and, in rural areas, to the TPA. The goal of the reform was to increase control over local decision-making. All these changes undermined the authority of the *raion* and *oblast* Party committees. Previously they, together with their soviet counterparts, had run the countryside. This gave rise to increasing opposition within the Party apparatus. In April 1964 Khrushchev complained that the TPAs were acting in the same way as the organizations they had replaced. This was not surprising since they were run by the same people, using the same work methods as before. The bewildering number of organizational changes, ill thought out and hastily implemented, condemned them to failure. In agriculture, as in industry, Khrushchev was always searching for the string which, if pulled, would set the Soviet economic mechanism functioning perfectly. Inevitably this was a fruitless search. Farms and farm labour needed to be stimulated through adjustments to the price mechanism. Even by 1964 animal husbandry was loss-making almost everywhere. This meant the more that was produced, the greater the loss to the farm.

In an attempt to recoup from the population some of the cost of the higher procurement prices the retail price of butter was increased by 25 per cent and that of meat by 30 per cent on 1 June 1962. Sugar dropped by 5 per cent but this did not assuage the sense of grievance felt by consumers. Price rises were a terrible shock to people used to fixed or even declining prices in the state sector. Tragedy struck in Novocherkassk where workers demonstrated and went on strike against the increases. Troops opened fire and a number of people were killed or injured.

Khrushchev changed almost all the ministers of agriculture at the centre and in the republics and replaced them with men who had a good track record as state farm managers. However, 1963 turned out to be disastrous. Two policies were adopted. First a crash programme was developed to expand the chemical industry to produce, among other things, mineral fertilizers and herbicides. This was no panacea for increased production as skilful choice of fertilizers was needed and they can be of limited value in dry farming areas due to the lack of moisture. The Soviet Union came late to the expansion of the chemical industry and the use of chemicals in agriculture. It was fortunate. Since then chemicals have caused appalling pollution in the USSR, mainly due to negligence. The other policy adopted was to import millions of tonnes of grain for cash from Canada, Australia and other countries. The Novocherkassk disturbances may have influenced the decision. It was a laudable one, nevertheless. Stalin would have let the population starve.

If the Soviet Union could not solve the problem of how to put more food, especially meat, on the table it was quite a different story in industry and space. There the country was bounding ahead. The Soviets had succeeded in landing a satellite on the moon and Khrushchev, during his American tour, proudly presented President Eisenhower with a copy of the pennant. That was nothing to the impact created by the first manned space flight on 12 April 1961. Yuri Gagarin became not only a hero at home but also abroad. Everyone wanted to meet him. A few months later German Tito spent twenty-five hours in space and orbited the earth seventeen times. The first group flight was made in August 1962 and in April 1963 Valentina Tereshkova became the first woman in space. It is interesting to note that to date she remains the only Soviet woman cosmonaut.

The US was left a long way behind. President Kennedy announced the Apollo mission whose goal was to put an American on the moon. The in-joke was that when the American landed he would be welcomed by a short, fat man, who would explain to him how to grow maize there.

US relations with Cuba deteriorated further under President John F. Kennedy. He inherited a plan for Cuban émigrés to invade, link up with the Cuban population and drive Castro out. The CIA and the émigrés got everything wrong and the Bay of Pigs invasion was routed with Castro leading his troops personally. An important factor in their defeat was the refusal of the US to provide air cover. Khrushchev immediately offered Cuba Soviet military aid. He only threatened the Americans after defeat of the invaders was certain. He sent Kennedy an insulting message afterwards in order to ram the Cuban victory home. Castro began to look round for a way to ensure that the Americans did not attempt another invasion. Soviet military advisers arrived in Cuba. The two countries had established diplomatic relations in February 1960. The Soviets at that time did not regard Fidel Castro as a communist although some of the leadership, such as his brother Raul and Ché Guevara, were.

There were setbacks for the Americans farther afield. The situation in Indo-China began to look ominous as Laos fell and South Vietnam looked fragile. The Soviets had made advances in the Middle East and Africa. They were breaking the ring of containment, which the Americans had built up, by establishing military bases around the world.

International developments seemed to be favouring Moscow and this put Kennedy under considerable pressure. He wanted to meet the Soviet leader and make his own assessment before he agreed to a summit meeting. Accordingly he invited Khrushchev to a meeting in a neutral country. The encounter took place in Vienna on 3–4 June 1961. There was no agenda and no communiqué was issued. Khrushchev was feeling on top of the world after Soviet achievements in space and the Cuban fiasco. Kennedy found the meeting 'sobering' and expected a 'cold winter'.

Addressing the Soviet people on 15 June Khrushchev put pressure on Kennedy. He reaffirmed the deadline for a Berlin settlement and indicated that he would sign a peace treaty with the GDR if the West refused an all-German treaty. The American's response was to announce on 25 July an increase in the US defence budget. Khrushchev reacted angrily and talked about the resumption of atomic testing and the explosion of a 100-megatonne bomb.

Academician Andrei Sakharov was alarmed by the prospects of a resumption of nuclear testing.

> I recall the summer of 1961, when a meeting had been arranged between Khrushchev ... and a number of atomic scientists. We were told that we had to prepare for a new series of tests, which were to provide support for the USSR's policy on the German question. I wrote a note to Khrushchev, saying: 'The revival of these tests after the three-year moratorium will be a breach of the test ban treaty and will check the move towards disarmament: it will lead to a fresh round in the arms race, especially in the sphere of inter-continental missiles and anti-missile defence.' I had this note passed along the rows of seats until it reach him. He put it in his breast pocket and invited all those present to dine with him ... he made an impromptu speech. This, more or less, is what he said: 'Sakharov is a good scientist, but he should leave foreign policy to those of us who are specialists in this subtle art. Strength alone can throw our enemy into confusion. We cannot say out loud that we base our policy on strength, but that is how it has to be'.[2]

Khrushchev either could not or would not match American increases in defence spending. He lowered his sights on Germany, and the East Germans, under Erich Honecker who at that time was Central Committee secretary for security, began to build the Berlin Wall on 13 August 1961. They demonstrated a sense of timing: 13 August was the anniversary of the birth of Karl Liebknecht, one of the founders of the Communist Party of Germany (KPD). The West was taken completely by surprise even though the GDR leader Walter Ulbricht had committed a·Freudian slip in replying to a question from a journalist. He categorically stated that there was no intention of building a wall – the question had not been about this subject. In his memoirs Khrushchev conceded that it had been necessary to 'guard the gates of the socialist paradise'. He conceded something about which the average Soviet citizen was absolutely unaware, 'Unfortunately, the GDR – and not only the GDR – has yet to reach a level of moral and material development where competition with the West is possible.'

Walter Ulbricht, the East German leader, was not satisfied with the Wall; he wanted the whole of Berlin. He had support within the Soviet leadership and the man regarded by many as the standard bearer of the hardline challenge to Khrushchev was Kozlov. Khrushchev and Kennedy exchanged conciliatory letters in October. Moscow dropped its demand for a 'troika' and accepted U Thant as the new UN secretary-general. At the Twenty-second Party Congress, in October 1961, a new wave of attacks on the 'Anti-Party group' was launched, suggesting there were still many doubters about de-Stalinization. Khrushchev needed to justify himself against the Chinese and Albanian challenge. He also withdrew the Berlin ultimatum but Walter Ulbricht argued strongly for a tough policy and the need for a peace treaty. He would not have done this without knowing that some in the Soviet leadership supported him.

The Cuban missile crisis

At the congress Marshal Malinovsky, the minister of defence, had reiterated the Soviet claim to military superiority. However, the US had by now perceived that there was no missile gap and was engaged in a strategic build-up which promised to give them a long lead in strategic missiles. Nikita Sergeevich was in a quandary. He had failed to browbeat the West into conceding a German treaty, the hostile Chinese would redouble their efforts to develop their own nuclear weapons, the strategic balance was tilting away from Moscow and the USSR did not have the resources to modernize its economy and engage in an expensive arms race.

Would the Americans have another try at removing Castro?

> I was haunted by the knowledge that the Americans could not stomach having Castro's Cuba right next door to them. Sooner or later the US would do something. It had the strength and it had the means ... How were we supposed to strengthen and reinforce Cuba? With diplomatic notes and TASS statements? The idea arose of placing our missile units in Cuba ... We concluded that we could send 42 missiles, each with a warhead of one megatonne. We picked targets in the US to inflict the maximum damage. We saw that our weapons could inspire terror. The two nuclear weapons the US used against Japan at the end of the war were toys by comparison.[3]

Would Castro accept the missiles? It immediately occurred to him that the nuclear weapons would not only protect Cuba but also all those fighting for socialism in the Third World. The Americans could be warned off if they tried to intervene. A treaty was negotiated and was ready for signing by late October 1962. However, events overtook the treaty and it was never signed. There is no record of the draft in the Soviet archives. However, the missiles were to be exclusively under Soviet control.

The Americans soon discovered what was afoot and on 18 October confronted Andrei Gromyko. Khrushchev records the response.

> Rusk (US Secretary of State) told Gromyko: 'We know everything.'
>
> Gromyko answered like a gypsy who's been caught

stealing a horse: 'It's not me, and it's not my horse. I don't know anything.'

Rusk said: 'We'll see this through to the end. Tell Khrushchev we wish we could prevent all this from occurring, but anything may happen.'[4]

On 22 October President Kennedy announced to the American people the discovery of the missiles on Cuba. He warned Khrushchev that any attack from Cuba would be the same as an attack from the USSR. He imposed a naval blockade or quarantine to prevent any more missiles being transported there. (However all the Soviet missiles were in place before 18 October.) Khrushchev takes up the story.

> Then we received a telegram from our ambassador in Cuba. He said that Castro claimed to have reliable information that the Americans were preparing within a certain number of hours to strike Cuba. Our own intelligence also informed us that an invasion would probably be unavoidable unless we came to an agreement with the President quickly. Castro suggested that to prevent our nuclear missiles being destroyed, we should launch a pre-emptive strike against the US.[5]

From 23–28 October Khrushchev and Kennedy exchanged letters. Kennedy warned that if Soviet missiles were not withdrawn action would be taken. Khrushchev argued that the missiles were there purely to protect Cuba and were therefore purely defensive. However, the possible seeds of a solution began to emerge. On 27 October, a US reconnaisance aircraft, flying at an altitude of 22,000 metres, was shot down over Cuba and the pilot killed. With the situation very tense Khrushchev, without consulting Castro, accepted the solution proposed by President Kennedy. Soviet missiles were to be removed from Cuba and, in return, the Americans, and their allies, would not invade Cuba. The first the Cubans heard of the decision to withdraw the missiles was a news broadcast on Soviet radio. Neither the Cubans nor the Soviet ambassador had been informed. It fell to Anastas Mikoyan to travel to Cuba to explain the Soviet decision. It was not an easy task.

> Castro was hotheaded. He thought we were retreating – worse, capitulating. He did not understand that our action was necessary to prevent a military confrontation. He also thought that America would not keep its word and once we had removed the missiles, the US would invade Cuba. He was very angry with us, but we accepted this with understanding.

These wounds were healed six months later when Castro landed in Murmansk to begin a triumphal forty-day tour of the Soviet Union. He was fêted everywhere and Nikita Sergeevich showed him around most of the time. He also spent time with the Khrushchevs and took photographs for the family album. Fidel looked the part of the revolutionary: tall, bearded and in military fatigues.

During the Cuban missile crisis the world came closer to nuclear war than at any time since 1945. The confrontation was almost inevitable given Khrushchev's exaggerated belief in nuclear weapons and the inevitable victory of communism. When he found the young American president unyielding he acted like a statesman and drew back from the brink. He had a horror of nuclear conflict and did not want war. His missiles, in the end, were bargaining pieces and were used in an attempt to strengthen Soviet security.

'The present generation of Soviet people will live under communism'

There were only two horses in the race to communism:

the Soviet and the Chinese. Mao Zedong had claimed that
China was ahead and this was one of the reasons behind
the 'Great Leap Forward'. Khrushchev had to outdo the
Chinese. He decided to present a new Party programme
but also to name the date when the USSR would enter
the glories of communism when everyone's needs would
be satisfied. The economic goals were extremely
ambitious as the Soviet Union in 1961 was a long way
behind the US, its role model. It assumed Soviet industrial growth of about 10 per cent annually, a vast expansion of agriculture and that the US economy was in
terminal decline. Based on these calculations the USSR
would surpass US gross and per capita production by
1970. A decade later and the USSR would have
constructed, in the main, a communist society, but when
1980 arrived the Soviet Union was in terminal decline.

In his never-ending search for the cadres to build a
community society – under his guidance – Nikita Sergeevich hit on a very useful notion. In the new Party rules it
was stated that at each regular congress one-quarter of
the members of the Central Committee (CC) and Presidium should be subject to deselection. Presidium
members were not, as a rule, to be elected for more than
three terms. Needless to say there were exceptions to
this rule. Those leaders who were indispensable could
stay on longer. The CCs of the republican Parties and
krai and *oblast* committees were to be renewed by not
less than a third at each regular election. Lower-level
bodies were to change half the personnel. This meant, in
practice, that an official could only serve a maximum of
six years at the bottom level and fifteen at the top. This
did not please those on the bottom rungs of the Party
apparatus. A Party post was no longer a job for life.

These changes resulted in a turnover in the Presidium
and CC at the congress. Among the three who lost their
Presidium places was N.G. Ignatov. He was very bitter
about his loss of status and this festered until he found

an outlet for his animus – coordinating opposition to Khrushchev. Only Khrushchev, Mikhail Suslov and Frol Kozlov survived as secretaries. Among the four new secretaries were Aleksandr Shelepin and Leonid Ilichev. Shelepin's place as head of the KGB went to Vladimir Semichastny.

A CC plenum in November introduced an even more unpopular reform – the bifurcation of the Party apparatus. There were to be two halves, one responsible for industry and the other charged with looking after agriculture. It was a clumsy reform and instead of improving the efficiency of the apparatus only caused frustration and discord. It was the first reform to be reversed after Khrushchev was removed in October 1964. A CC plenum in November 1962 elected Yuri Andropov a CC secretary and Leonid Ilichev was made chairman of the Ideological Commission which was attached to the CC. He became a guardian of socialist realism and gained a reputation as an arch conservative in cultural affairs. He had a baleful influence on Khrushchev's views. Ilichev is a fascinating study as he was a pillar of orthodoxy who harmed many artistic careers. However, in private, he was an avid collector of avant garde art.

As the economy became more complex so new state committees were established to supervise every sector. The government became so large that it resembled a maze. An official needed a chart to find his way around the bureaucracy.

The Twenty-second Party Congress returned to the problem of the Stalin legacy. Khrushchev spoke of the 'Anti-Party group' and named them all for the first time. He went on:

> Initially it was Molotov, Kaganovich, Malenkov and Voroshilov who resisted most forcefully the Party's policy, which was to condemn the cult of personality, to foster inner-Party democracy, to condemn and

redress all abuses of power and to.expose those who were directly responsible for the elaboration and implementation of repressive measures.[7]

Speaker after speaker vied to expose even more heinous crimes by those already condemned. Kaganovich was a 'degenerate' who should have been expelled from the Party. Malenkov should also be expelled as well and so on. Other revelations about the abuses of power in the late 1930s caused a sensation. Khrushchev provided more gory details and it was agreed to erect a monument to Stalin's victims. One of the most remarkable speeches was by D. Lazurkina, who had spent seventeen years in the gulag. She informed incredulous delegates that Vladimir Ilich Lenin had appeared to her and made it quite clear that he did not like lying beside Stalin in the mausoleum. After this message from the other world, delegates had to agree to the removal of Stalin's body. They did not have the nerve to take it away and dispose of it but buried it near the mausoleum. Later a headstone with the inscription: I.V. Stalin was erected. It is still there.

All this annoyed many CC members. It made it impossible to ignore the subject of Stalin's crimes. Inevitably the key question was: who was responsible? Practically everyone in the apparatus was responsible, at least, in part. Maurice Thorez, the conservative French Party leader, argued forcibly that the exposures of the trials of the 1930s and all the other repressions should be handled with greater care. Otherwise the world communist movement would be greatly damaged. Thorez was appealing after the horse had bolted. The revelations about Stalin mortally wounded the world movement. Khrushchev did not take the next logical step: rehabilitate those who had lost out in the factional infighting against Stalin. It would be left to Gorbachev to bring Bukharin, for instance, in from the cold.

The whole cultural climate changed, with those who

had suffered beginning to put pen to paper. In 1962 books and articles and a large number of memoirs were published. Evegenia Ginzburg's *Into the Whirlwind* is a profoundly moving account of her travails. One of the most influential novels was Aleksandr Solzhenitsyn's *One Day in the Life of Ivan Denisovich*. It was published in the literary journal *Novy Mir*. The editor, Aleksandr Tvardovsky, felt unable to judge whether it should be published and forwarded a copy to Khrushchev. Copies were also given to members of the Presidium.

I wish I'd handled the Pasternak affair the way I dealt with Aleksandr Solzhenitsyn's *One Day in the Life of Ivan Denisovich*. In that case, I read the book myself. [In reality it was read to him by an aide, V.A. Lebedev.] It is very heavy but well written. It made the reader react with revulsion to the conditions in which Ivan Denisovich and his friends lived while they served their terms. Only Suslov squawked. He wanted to hold everything in check. 'You can't do this!' he said. 'That's all there is to it. How will the people under-stand?' My answer then and now is that people will always distinguish good from bad. In deciding not to interfere with Solzhenitsyn's book, I proceeded from the premise that the evil inflicted on the Communist Party and on the Soviet people had to be condemned; we had to lance the boil, to brand what had happened with shame so that it would never happen again. We had to brand the truth into literature. Readers really devoured Solzhenitsyn's book. They were trying to find out how an honest man could end up in such conditions in our socialist time and our socialist state.[8]

Suslov, Ilichev and other conservative bureaucrats were alarmed by the flowering of unofficial culture. They decided what represented culture. There was a cultural mafia in operation and it looked after its own. If the

liberal wave continued they ran the risk of becoming
redundant. An exhibition of modern art was arranged for
Khrushchev's eyes when he visited the Manège in
Moscow on 1 December 1962. Ernst Neizvestny, a
talented sculptor, records what happened:

[Khrushchev] began his inspection in the room where
paintings by Bilyutin and some other friends of mine
had been hung. He swore horribly and became
extremely angry about them. It was there that he said
a 'donkey could do better with his tail' and remarked
of Zhukovsky that he was a handsome man but drew
monsters ... Khrushchev said I devoured the people's
money and produced shit. I told him he knew nothing
about art ... And I told him the confrontation had been
staged, that it was a plot to undermine not only liberal-
isation, not just the intelligentsia, not just me – but
also him. It seemed to me that my point struck home,
though he went on denouncing me and my work ... He
said: 'You're an interesting man – I enjoy people like
you – but inside you are an angel and a devil. If the
devil wins, we'll crush you. If the angel wins, we'll do
all we can to help you.' And he held out his hand.[9]

Khrushchev's son, Sergei Nikitich, tries to explain his
father's reaction:

Father could discuss issues relating to agriculture,
construction, and defence for hours; here he was in his
element. The problem of 'bourgeois ideological infil-
tration' was utterly foreign to him, but the thirties and
forties had ingrained in him a hardline algorithm
dictating that such things must be mercilessly resisted.
And he threw himself into the fight. Sculpture and the
fine arts in general constituted a 'theatre of military
action', and the confrontation at the Manège was one
episode in the ideological battle. The plan was to use

father himself to crush the upstart intellectuals. Unfortunately, the plan was a success.[10]

At a gathering of cultural workers on 8 March 1963 Khrushchev spoke of Stalin's 'services' to the Party and his 'devotion' to Marxism and communism. He had been ill towards the end of his life and suffered from paranoia. His crimes were due to his illness. It was dangerous to treat Stalin's crimes in contemporary literature. This put an end to this type of literature. Was this volte-face due to political pressure or did he think that demolishing Stalin would eventually risk demolishing the Party?

The life of the believer improved after Khrushchev's denunciation of Stalin and church life was more normal in 1959 than at any time since the revolution. Then began a vicious campaign of persecution which saw ten thousand churches and dozens of monasteries closed. The Monastery of the Caves, in Kiev, the most sacred place of the Orthodox faith, was one of them. Believers were harassed and imprisoned. It is still a mystery why Khrushchev singled out the church, a soft target, for such treatment. He passed *One Day in the Life of Ivan Denisovich* for publication, yet it contains two memorable portraits of Christian believers in it. Khrushchev made it clear that under communism there was no room for religion. Perhaps it was Suslov or Ilichev or other dogmatists who provoked him into doing something to stem the rise of religious belief in the Soviet Union. It remains a disgraceful episode, not only because it denied freedom of conscience, but because it also destroyed part of Russia's cultural heritage.

Decline and Fall, 1963-64 5

As Khrushchev got older so the duties of office became even heavier. His son records him coming home, going for his usual walk, eating and then settling down until midnight with some files. He was back in the office at nine the next morning. He travelled very widely, partly because he was insatiably curious about the world but also because he was always looking for better ways of doing things. In his last year of office he travelled a remarkable amount. This allowed the opposition to consolidate and plan his downfall.

He committed some grave errors. In May 1964 he and his entourage went to Egypt and were fêted by Nasser and the Egyptian people. While there he helped inaugurate the Aswan High Dam. Agreements on economic aid and cooperation were negotiated and Nasser conferred on Khrushchev his country's highest decoration, the Necklace of the Nile. This put the Soviet leader in a quandary. Nasser and Marshal Hakim Amer, commander-in-chief of the armed forces, could hardly be given the Order of Lenin. The highest Soviet decoration, according to the USSR Supreme Soviet Presidium, was Hero of the Soviet Union. So Nasser was decorated by Khrushchev and at Marshal Grechko's suggestion Marshal Amer was also. Andrei Gromyko nodded his approval. The awards were a mistake. Nasser and Amer had supported Nazi Germany during the war. Apparently Khrushchev announced the decision before it had been presented to the Party Presidium. The Soviet leader did not place great store by medals, awards and presents but others did. He did not take this into consideration. He also ignored the fact that Nasser dealt very roughly with his communists.

Khrushchev was oblivious to the fact that he was undermining his own position. Clearly he regarded his posts as his for life. He had survived under Stalin by deploying great inter-personal skills. Now he neglected them or forgot them. A typical example was his trip to Poland in January 1964. He took along Kiril Mazurov, Party leader in Belorussia, whom he admired. They fell out over economic policy and when Khrushchev arrived back in Moscow he told the Presidium that a way would have to be found to remove Mazurov. This did not happen but it turned Mazurov against Khrushchev.

He first openly talked about retiring during the celebrations surrounding his 70th birthday in April 1964. He had no one particular in mind to succeed him. Had Frol Kozlov not suffered a stroke in April 1963 he might have been his choice, even though Kozlov belonged to the conservative wing of the Presidium.

The campaign to remove him, according to Vladimir Semichastny, head of the KGB at the time, began in February 1964. Its genesis may have been the CC plenum in February. Podgorny, Brezhnev, Shelepin and Polyansky were the conspirators. Their task of discrediting Khrushchev was made easier by Nikita Sergeevich's blundering leadership. In August he visited the Virgin Lands of Kazakhstan and again fell out with Baraev over fallow. Very angry, he dismissed him. When he had gone the Party leader of the region convened his bureau and it found in favour of Baraev. He was reinstated. In September Khrushchev proposed the setting up of special organizations which would supervise all the major sectors of agriculture. It encountered strong opposition in the Party Presidium and among obkom first secretaries. These two incidents may be related. This type of open dissent had been unprecedented since 1957. They may have been encouraged by the CC Secretariat.

Pyotr Shelest, member of the Presidium and Party leader in the Ukraine, dates the conspiracy from 14 March 1964, his birthday. Podgorny and Brezhnev drove over to congratulate him.

> I had a premonition ... They didn't quite trust me. They were sounding me out.[1]

Soundings were being taken. Simultaneously the cult of Khrushchev's personality reached new heights. His portraits got bigger, he was quoted as an authority on everything. Then the film *Our Nikita Sergeevich* was put on general release. Albums tracing Khrushchev's life were published. Podgorny and Brezhnev vied with one another to be sycophant of the month. During Khrushchev's 70th birthday reception eulogies to his wisdom reached new heights. Brezhnev made the main speech. Everyone else followed. It was reminiscent of the Stalin era.

The incapacitation of Kozlov led to Brezhnev being drafted into the CC Secretariat while remaining state president. When it became clear Kozlov would never return Khrushchev decided to move Brezhnev full time into the Secretariat and make Anastas Mikoyan president. This annoyed Brezhnev who loved the trappings of presidential office. So keen was he to remain in office that it would appear that he tried to arrange the removal of Khrushchev there and then. According to Semichastny, Brezhnev came up with various ways of eliminating Nikita Sergeevich. One was by administering poison. The idea of

113

causing the plane bringing him back from Cairo to crash was also canvassed. Brezhnev though of arranging a car accident for Khrushchev. Another desperate plan was mooted – arrest Nikita Sergeevich on the train coming back from Sweden.

At the Supreme Soviet meeting in July Khrushchev wanted to introduce the five-day week. The conspirators feared this might make him popular so they set about dissuading him. Aleksei Adzhubei, his son-in-law and editor-in-chief of *Izvestiya*, finally convinced him the moment was not opportune. Unwittingly Adzhubei had helped the opposition.

Then everyone went off on vacation to the Crimea. Brezhnev, now 'second' secretary and Khrushchev's deputy, went too. It was a golden opportunity to talk to Party officials, especially those in the Central Committee. Practically everyone was unhappy with Khrushchev. Among those Brezhnev approached again was Shelest.

> He didn't try to persuade me. He just sobbed, actually burst into tears. The man was an actor, a great actor. It sometimes got to the point, when he'd downed a few drinks, that he'd climb on a chair and declaim something or other. Not Mayakovsky, of course, or Esenin, but some pun he'd thought up ... '[Khrushchev] swears at us, says we don't do a damn thing.' Brezhnev sounded hurt, and there were tears in his eyes ... We're thinking of calling a plenum and criticizing him a little. So what's the problem? Count me in favour.[2]

Brezhnev was a very keen hunter and enjoyed duck shooting at Zavidovo, outside Moscow. However, in August 1964 his mind was not on the duck, it was on power. Gennady Voronov, then a member of the Presidium, sets the scene:

Everything had been under preparation for about a year. The threads led to Zavidovo, where Brezhnev usually went hunting. Brezhnev himself would put down a plus (next to the names of those who were ready to support him in the fight against Khrushchev) or minus. Each man would be worked on individually.[3]

In September Khrushchev went off to inspect some military hardware but his son, Sergei Nikitich, fell ill at the last moment and could not accompany him. He received a telephone call from Vasily Galyukov, an associate of Nikolai Ignatov, who had lost his position in the Presidium some years previously. The associate informed Sergei Nikitich that Ignatov was involved in a conspiracy against his father. In Sochi, in August, he had had many meetings with Party officials. Ignatov always reported to Brezhnev.

Sergei Nikitich informed his father when he returned.

'Tell me again, whom did the man mention by name?' he asked.

Ignatov, Podgorny, Brezhnev, Shelepin ... I began to repeat them, trying to be as precise as possible.

Father thought for a moment.

'No, it's incredible. Brezhnev, Podgorny, Shelepin – they're completely different people. It can't be,' he said thoughtfully. 'Ignatov – that's possible. He's very dissatisfied, and he's not a good man anyway. But what can he have in common with the others?'[4]

The topic came up again the following evening.

'Evidently, what you told me is nonsense. I was leaving the Council of Ministers with Mikoyan and Podgorny, and I summarised your story in a couple of words. Podgorny simply laughed at me. "How can you think

115

such a thing, Nikita Sergeevich?" Those were his actual words.'[5]

Khrushchev's naïvety is staggering. The obvious thing to have done was to ask Mikoyan to look into the allegations and report back. Nikita Sergeevich's political skills had clearly deserted him. His son suggests the following explanation.

Only much later did I understand the sources of my father's behaviour. He did not believe, he did not want to believe, that such a turn of events was possible. After all, the people accused had been his friends for decades! If he couldn't trust them, whom could he trust? What's more, my seventy-year-old father was tired, tired beyond measure, both morally and physically. He had neither the strength nor the desire to fight for power. Let everything take its course. I won't interfere, he had obviously decided.[6]

He went off with Mikoyan to Pitsunda in the Crimea for a rest. On 12 October a space launch was planned and Leonid Smirnov, the deputy prime minister responsible for missile technology, was, as usual, expected to phone immediately the spacecraft was in orbit. He didn't phone. Khrushchev got agitated and phoned him, berating him for being inefficient. It was clear that as far as the deputy prime minister was concerned the transfer of power to Brezhnev and his co-conspirators had already taken place.

Mikhail Suslov phoned Khrushchev in the evening and told him the Presidium had convened and requested his presence. Under protest he agreed but confided to Mikoyan that if he was the issue, he would go quietly.

Brezhnev was on a visit to East Germany when he was told that Khrushchev had got wind of the plot. He did not want to return. He was to have phoned Khrushchev. 'It wasn't easy to talk him into it,' remarked Semichastny, 'we had practically to drag him to the phone.' However, at the last moment he backed down. Suslov took over. He had only been apprised of the *coup* a week previously since he was neither a member of the Brezhnev–Podgorny group nor the Shelepin group. When he was told of it he pursed his lips until they were blue and sucked in his cheeks. 'What are you talking about? That means civil war,' he responded. He soon joined. Aleksei Kosygin was also told at the very end, according to Semichastny:

> When they came to Kosygin about a week before, his first question was:
> 'Where does the KGB stand?' When they told him that we were on board, he said: 'It's fine with me.'
> As for Malinovsky, he was told with two days to go ... with only two days to go ...!! Can you imagine that?[7]

Khrushchev had one last official duty to perform. On the morning of 13 October, at Pitsunda, he received Gaston Palewski, the French minister, but for only half an hour.

Khrushchev and Mikoyan were met at Vnukovo 2 airport by Semichastny. He informed Nikita Sergeevich that everyone was waiting for him at the Kremlin.

Why was it Semichastny, the KGB chief, who met him?

> In the morning I called Leonid Ilich. Who's going to go to meet him? I asked.
> 'No one. You go by yourself,' he replied. How can that be? I stammered. 'Under the present circumstances,' he said slowly, 'why should everyone go?' On the whole he was right ... But won't he catch on? I asked a little worriedly. 'Just take some security and go,' Brezhnev said, ending the conversation.[8]

Semichastny had taken some other precautions.

I didn't even close the Kremlin to visitors. People were strolling around outside, while ... in the room the Presidium was meeting. I deployed my men around the Kremlin. Everything that was necessary was done. Brezhnev and Shelepin were nervous. I told them: Let's not do anything that isn't necessary. Let's not create the appearance of a *coup*.[9]

That evening Brezhnev still felt nervous. He called Semichastny.

'Volodya, the meeting has just ended. Khrushchev is leaving. Where is he going?' To his flat. 'But if he heads for his dacha?' Let him go to his dacha. 'If he does that, what will you do?' I've got everything ready, here, there and everywhere. We've anticipated everything. 'What if he phones? What if he calls in help?' He's got no place to call. The whole communications network is in my hands ... I've got the Kremlin lines, and the Party lines. If he wants to use the ordinary city phone, let him.[10]

The minutes of the meeting of the Presidium, chaired by Khrushchev, have been lost, apparently destroyed deliberately. However the minutes of the Central Committee plenum which dismissed Khrushchev do exist.

It is uncertain when Nikita Sergeevich decided to go. During the night of 13–14 October he phoned Mikoyan and said that he would not object if he were deprived of his offices.

I'm old and tired. Let them cope by themselves. I've done the main thing. Relations among us, the style of leadership, has changed drastically. Could anyone have dreamt of telling Stalin that he didn't suit us anymore, and suggesting that he retire? Not even a wet spot would have remained where we had been standing. Now everything is different. The fear's gone and we can talk as equals. That's my contribution. I won't put up a fight.[11]

However, Pyotr Shelest kept his own record of the Presidium proceedings. Khrushchev was 'dispirited and isolated'. However, he tried to answer his critics.

'The Party brought up and educated all of us, including me. We owe our political situation to it and it alone. You and I stand on common political and ideological ground, so I cannot fight you. I'll step down. I don't intend to fight. I ask you to forgive me if I ever offended anyone, if I allowed myself to behave rudely ... I just want to say that I categorically reject some of the accusations made against me ... you, all of you present here, didn't tell me openly and honestly about my shortcomings. You were all yes men ... I understand that this is my last political speech, my swan song, so to speak. I shall not appear before the plenum, but I'd like to make one request to the plenum ...'

He didn't manage to say [Shelest records] what his request was before Brezhnev cut him off. 'There will be no request.' Suslov supported Brezhnev. Tears appeared in Nikita Sergeevich's eyes, and then he simply broke down and cried. It was sad to see ... Polyansky had prepared the report to the plenum. The idea was for Brezhnev to give it, or at the very least, Podgorny. But Brezhnev simply funked it. And Podgorny also refused ... 'I'd suggest Shelepin. He's got a way with words but he's too young.' Then it was decided this way: 'Let Mikhail Andreevich [Suslov] give it. After all, he's our ideologist.'[12]

Semichastny advised Brezhnev to cut the Presidium proceedings short.

'All this criticism is going on too long,' I said. 'Get it over with. I couldn't stand another night of it. At the rate you're going, Leonid Ilich, you'll keep meeting until they arrest either you or Khrushchev. I don't need that.'[13]

The CC plenum met on 14 October, beginning at 6 p.m. Semichastny was surprised that there was no discussion. He was annoyed at the time but came to see the wisdom of it later.

The Presidium decided everything for the Central Committee, and having decided, prepared, chewed it over, and then chewed it over again, and threw it to the CC, saying, 'Vote!'[14]

The Presidium report, delivered by Suslov, indicted Khrushchev on fifteen counts. It was the prosecution's case. There was not a word of thanks or praise for Nikita Sergeevich.

Among other things, he was accused of providing erratic leadership; of taking hasty and ill-considered decisions; of ignoring and slighting his colleagues; of developing his own personality cult; of turning Aleksei Adzhubei into a shadow foreign minister but he was 'obsequious, incompetent and irresponsible' and had insulted Walter Ulbricht, the East German leader; the bifurcation of the Party apparatus had caused much confusion; he had regarded himself as an expert on everything he came in contact with; industrial administration had become very complex and unwieldy; his policies had undermined the welfare of the workers; he was often insensitive in dealing with foreign affairs and thereby exacerbated tensions – he referred once, for example, to Mao Zedong as an 'old boot'; on another occasion, he told Todor Zhivkov, the Bulgarian leader, that all Bulgarians were parasites; he damaged foreign trade relations and never met or telephoned the minister of foreign trade; his campaigns against fallow and peasants' private plots and his support for the charlatan Lysenko had cost agriculture dear; and he had promised and disbursed too much largesse to Third World states. Many of these criticisms were justified.

Mikoyan came to see Khrushchev to inform him about his future. The city flat and dacha were to be his for life. New bodyguards and domestic staff were to be assigned to him. He was to have a 500 ruble a month pension and a car. Mikoyan had suggested that Khrushchev be appointed consultant to the Presidium but not surprisingly this was turned down. Before leaving Mikoyan embraced Nikita Sergeevich and kissed him. They parted. They were never to meet again.

The Unhappy Pensioner, 1964-71

6

Nikita Sergeevich's dismissal wounded him mortally. He was never able to come to terms with the shock of having his life's work overturned and the disgrace of becoming an 'unperson'. A very sensitive person, the dull weight of rejection crushed his spirit until his dying day. Even the devoted care of his wife, Nina Petrovna, was not able to reduce the pain. She suffered as much as he did but was better able to conceal it. Arbat, his daughter's Alsatian, knew while Nikita Sergeevich was in office that he had no time for him. When Khrushchev returned after his dismissal Arbat went up to him and thereafter never left his side. The dog sensed that he now had all the time in the world for him.

Khrushchev had been dismissed while three Soviet cosmonauts were in orbit and he had promised them a hero's welcome when they landed. The festivities took place on 23 October. Khrushchev found he could not watch it on television and took off for his dacha. However, Brezhnev and the others feared the worst – he was heading for Red Square! The panic subsided when the car changed direction and made for the dacha. Brezhnev ensured that there would be no repeat of the episode. Nikita Sergeevich was requested to move immediately to his dacha and not to come back to Moscow. The family were at liberty to stay in the capital but would have to move to another flat.

Brezhnev summoned him to the Central Committee to tell him what the conditions were under which he was to live. It was to be their last meeting. One of them was that he was to move to another, more modest, dacha in the country, at Petrovo-Dalnee. Both his Moscow flat and the dacha were bugged. It was all quite amateurish. The guards were bored so they played music tapes but the microphones in the walls became speakers. The walls were alive to the sound of music!

The family became alarmed at Nikita Sergeevich's pessimism. He kept on repeating bitterly that his life was over, that life made sense only as long as people needed him. No one needed him now, so life was meaningless. His doctor explained that this was one of the symptoms of shock.

Talk about the memoirs began in 1966. With all the time in the world and with such a wealth of experience he was ideally suited to write about his life and times. But Nikita Sergeevich never picked up a pen if he could help it. The invention of the tape recorder solved the problem. Judicious questioning could unleash a store of information and insights. Khrushchev loved meeting people and talking and could not bear to be alone. At the dacha it was often difficult to drag him into a conversation, so low were his spirits. The driving force behind the project was his son, Sergei Nikitich. Khrushchev refused to seek official aid, the use of a stenographer and so on. He was right. The authorities would have killed the project in its infancy. To begin with, he did not want to dictate inside because he would be broadcasting everything to the KGB. Outside also proved unsuitable because of overflying aircraft. In the end he moved back inside and thereby kept the KGB well informed. They did not prohibit his activities since they had no order to do so. Reports were passed up the line and considered. Surprisingly some time passed before attempts were made to scupper the whole operation.

Transcribing and editing eventually became the responsibility of Sergei Nikitich. Khrushchev dictated from memory – a phenomenal memory – and did not rely on sources. Especially startling were his recollections of the war: he hardly got a fact wrong. This revealed how deeply the experience had engraved itself on his memory. He dictated best when he had an old acquaintance in front of him. He planned carefully. He went for long walks to think over the best way of saying something. He avoided a chronological account and so flitted from topic to topic.

By 1968 Brezhnev was feeling sufficiently sure of himself to try to silence Khrushchev. He had no desire to meet Khrushchev again personally so Andrei Kirilenko was given the job. Arvid Pelshe, chairman of the Party Control Commission (the Party's own police) and Pyotr Demichev, another senior official, sat in to add gravity to the situation. Khrushchev was summoned to the CC building. Kirilenko, who would have won first prize for rudeness in the Politburo, came over very heavy. Hand over the memoirs and stop dictating. A mere pensioner has no right to write the history of the Party and state.

Nikita Sergeevich categorically refused, getting more angry by the minute.

'You can take everything away from me: my pension, the dacha, my flat. That's all within your power, and it wouldn't surprise me if you did. So what – I can still make a living. I'll go back to being a metalworker – I still remember how it's done. If that doesn't work out, I'll put on my rucksack and go begging. People will give me what I need.'

He looked at Kirilenko. 'But no one would give you a

crust of bread. You'd starve ... you violated the constitution ... when you stuck listening devices all over the
dacha. Even in the toilet – you spend the people's
money eavesdropping on my farts.'[1]

His volcanic anger slowly subsided but Kirilenko, who
was no match for him, scored a partial victory. Nikita
Sergeevich recorded very little in 1968. The episode so
alarmed him that he began to discuss ways of getting the
tapes and transcripts abroad. They could be published in
retaliation for some action, if need be. It turned out to be
relatively simple to get them into a foreign bank vault.
Those passages regarded as too inflammatory were
excised from the first American edition in 1971. These
were published in 1990.

Brezhnev and the KGB did not give up. They tried
various techniques to extract them from Sergei Nikitich.
They hoped to catch him with all the material on him. He
was warned about foreign agents trying to steal the
memoirs and an American medical contact was given a
tough time. By this time Yuri Andropov had taken over as
KGB head. Sergei Nikitich had some faith in him and
eventually agreed to hand over the material on 11 July
1970. There were 2,810 typewritten pages and the typists
had a further 929. His father was in hospital and it was
agreed that the materials would be returned when he left
hospital. This never materialized as the KGB stated that
everything had been passed to the Central Committee at
its request. Sergei Nikitich had been neatly out-
manoeuvred. Nikita Sergeevich never forgave his son for
turning over the materials to the KGB.

Then it was announced that the memoirs would be
published in the US. Nikita Sergeevich was hauled in front
of Arvid Pelshe. Eventually he signed a statement that his
memoirs were not complete and that he had not sent
them abroad. Both statements were technically correct. The
official business over, he could not resist the temptation

to pour scorn on the limited achievements of his successors. He took considerable pleasure in pointing out that Soviet agriculture was in such a state that grain had to be imported annually from the US! He had not come to debate but to pour out his frustration and the pain he felt at the lack of innovative leadership then so evident. It was as if all his ideals had been betrayed. Nikita Sergeevich had to pay a price for his outburst. He suffered a mild heart attack and had to return to hospital. When he returned home at the end of 1970 a rapid decline set in. He could no longer walk very far without resting on a folding stool he always took with him. Arbat had carried it but he was now gone. He began dictating again in February but it was not the old Khrushchev. He was dissatisfied with his recollections about cultural policy.

In January 1971 the KGB had called Sergei Nikitich in and invited him to check a Russian retranslation of the English published edition. This seemed strange since they could surely have checked the retranslation against the original Russian in the possession of the Central Committee. The American version was much shorter – much of the war material had been omitted. Progress Publishers then brought out the Russian translation and it was stamped for 'official use only'. Hence the Soviet establishment became aware of what Khrushchev had said.

When Volume Two of the memoirs came out in America in 1974 Sergei Nikitich was again contacted by the KGB. They wanted him to sign a letter declaring the memoirs to be a forgery. This posed a slight difficulty since he had not seen the second volume. He consulted his mother, Nina Petrovna, and she pointed out logically that one could not state that the book was a forgery if one had not read it. This was reported to the KGB. Sergei Nikitich demanded to see a copy for himself and his mother. The KGB conceded that they had not seen a copy either! So a letter was signed which amounted to no more than what his father had conceded to Pelshe: the memoirs were incomplete and he had no idea how they had ended up abroad.

When Brezhnev died in November 1982 Sergei Nikitich thought of asking his successor, Yuri Andropov, to return the tapes and transcripts. When he finally got round to sending a letter, Mikhail Gorbachev was leader. He agreed very quickly to their return. This was more easily said than done. Almost two years passed and still the materials had not reappeared. There were the usual excuses: the archives were undergoing restoration; they were being moved to another building; and so on. Finally, in August 1988 came the exciting news: they were ready. However, disappointment was in store. Only four hundred pages were in the folder. What about the rest? [It transpired that the Central Committee was holding about six thousand pages.] Promises were made to look into the matter.

Glasnost helped to solve the problem. The American publishers *Time* returned all the materials they had to Sergei Nikitich. Other sources had been hidden away in the Soviet Union. Work began on the definitive Russian edition of the memoirs.

Farewell

Khrushchev's seventy-seventh birthday was celebrated at Petrovo-Dalnee on 17 April 1971. He was in a sombre mood as his doctor had forbidden him to do any gardening. It had been one of his delights. Many of his agricultural innovations had first been tried out in his garden. It was the last family gathering at Petrovo-Dalnee. In July black melancholy overtook Nikita Sergeevich and he spoke of suicide.

On 5 September he and Nina Petrovna intended to visit their daughter Rada, her husband Aleksei Adzhubei and the family. But his heart began to trouble him.

During the night, in hospital, he suffered a massive heart attack. He died on 11 September 1971.

Central Committee officials confiscated from the dacha all Khrushchev's private papers and other materials which they regarded as important. The CC also decided that Khrushchev's death would be announced at 10 a.m. on Monday 13 September, the wake would begin at the same time in a suburban hospital and the funeral would be at noon in Novodevichy Cemetery. This would ensure that many who wished to attend would hear too late to be there. The CC would also pay all funeral expenses. No one from the Politburo phoned his condolences. It was as if Khrushchev had never lived. But they were relieved that the Soviet Union's number one dissident was dead.

Khrushchev remained a Party member to his dying day. The CC sent a wreath: 'To Comrade N.S. Khrushchev from the CC, CPSU and the USSR Council of Ministers.' One arrived at the very last moment: 'To Nikita Sergeevich Khrushchev from Anastas Ivanovich Mikoyan.' His son, Sergo, had not informed him of Khrushchev's death. He learnt about it from that morning's *Pravda.* Had he known about the funeral he might have wanted to attend. That would have been very embarrassing for the authorities.

Nina Petrovna Khrushchev was moved to a dacha in Zhukovka. The one in Petrovo-Dalnee was demolished. No physical trace was to be left of Khrushchev's existence. She always expressed a wish to be buried beside her husband. When she died in August 1984 Konstantin Chernenko was Party leader – no use approaching him for permission. Fortunately he was on holiday at the time and Mikhail Gorbachev was in charge in Moscow. A request was made and permission was given within ninety minutes.

All trace of Khrushchev disappeared except his grave. Sergei Nikitich determined to erect a headstone which would also serve as a monument. He was advised that the only sculptor who could do justice to the subject was Ernst Neizvestny. He hesitated about approaching the artist since he and his father had rowed furiously at the Manège. He need not have worried. Neizvestny respected his father for his achievements. But how was he going to represent the successes and failures?

In a philosophical sense, life itself is based on antagonism between two principles. One is bright, progressive, dynamic; the other is dark, reactionary, static. One strains to move forward, the other pulls back. This basic idea fits Nikita Sergeevich's image quite well. He began to lead our country out of the darkness and he exposed Stalin's crimes. The dawn broke for all of us, heralding the imminent rise of the sun. Light began to dispel the darkness.

This approach helps us to understand the basic ideas reflected in the monument. The main component is white marble, its dynamic form bearing down on black granite. The darkness resists, struggles, refuses to yield – as with man himself. It's no accident that the head is on a white pedestal, or that the background remains dark. In the upper corner of the white is a symbolic representation of the sun. Rays extend down from it, dispelling the darkness. The head, the colour of old gold on white, not only pleases the eye, it's also a symbol ... It all rests on the sturdy foundation of a bronze slab. It can't be budged. There's no reversing the process which has begun. On the left of the slab, seen from the stele, there's a heart-shaped aperture. Red flowers ought to grow there, to symbolize enthusiasm and self-sacrifice.[2]

Permission to erect the monument was given by Aleksei Kosygin. It had needed a prime minister to decide whether it could be erected. In September 1975, after four years of endeavour, it was finally in place. The artist's name caused some confusion. Those who do not know of him are puzzled when they read: Artist: Unknown. Neizvestny means unknown in Russian. They are bemused to be told that Mr Unknown is very well known worldwide.

Nikita Sergeevich and Mikhail Sergeevich

Khrushchev failed and was brushed aside. His successors pretended he had not been. Will the same thing happen to Gorbachev?

Without Khrushchev there would have been no Gorbachev. Nikita Sergeevich broke the Stalinist ice but the current of reform was not strong enough. The ice reformed. But many were touched by the post-1956 world. It planted seeds which are only bearing fruit today. Gorbachev was one of Khrushchev's offspring.

Khrushchev addressed all the major problems facing Soviet society today. He emphasized the need for economic self-interest. This led to the abolition of the all-embracing central ministries. The *sovnarkhozy* were not the solution to the problem of locating decision-making nearer the point of production. However, they were a step in the right direction. Enterprises had to gain greater control over their activities and this led Khrushchev to toy with the idea of a socialist market. In agriculture he was aware that increased investment was not the solution. The key was the attitude of the farm worker. He could not accept that the family farm was a better vehicle than the collective or state farm. He remained a child of the 1930s. He battled with the armed forces to reduce military spending. He set peaceful co-existence in train but thought that exploding the world's largest nuclear device would force the West into granting the Soviet Union parity.

Gorbachev is able to look back on the Khrushchev era and draw lessons from it. Khrushchev and he share fundamental beliefs: both leaders are Leninists who are convinced that an advanced socialist society can be built. Mikhail Sergeevich, like Khrushchev, believes he is indispensable and possesses insights that others lack. They are centralists, thinking that a strong centre holds out the best prospects for successful reform. Gorbachev is more radical than Khrushchev since the situation is much worse. He, like Khrushchev, came to see that the Party apparat is a great barrier to progress. Gorbachev has taken some steps in the direction of a market economy but has retained the economic ministries and control over most prices. He prefers cooperatives with the state a major shareholder. He is not convinced that private enterprise is good for the Soviet Union. The state monopoly of transport and distribution has hardly been touched. Gorbachev, like Khrushchev, has agonized about defence spending. The country cannot sustain the present burden. There is one problem which Gorbachev inherited which caused Khrushchev little trouble – the nationalities problem. Khrushchev was aware of the injustices of Stalin's rule and rehabilitated all those people accused of treachery during the war and deported. He also adopted positive discrimination, believing that the new non-Russian elites would accept Russian leadership in the building of communism. He was wrong and Gorbachev has reaped the whirlwind.

Khrushchev, in retirement, accepted that the main thrust of his cultural policy was wrong. It was too negative. Gorbachev has taken this much further and *glasnost* and democratization have transformed the Soviet Union. Gorbachev's courting of the churches, especially the Orthodox Church, would have shocked Nikita Sergeevich. Khrushchev began opening the window to the outside world. He travelled extensively with his family and Gorbachev has followed suit.

Gorbachev is a more skilled politician than Khrushchev. He is capable of putting together tactical alliances and outmanoeuvring his opponents. He never forgets that each victory is merely the prelude to the next battle. Khrushchev enjoyed greater authority among the people. He was held in affection in a way that Gorbachev is not.

Both leaders have had to wrestle with more or less the same problems. Neither found solutions to some of the fundamental issues facing Soviet society. It may be that the future will reveal that Khrushchev broke out of darkness into light, proceeded a short way forward and that Gorbachev continued the journey until the road ran out. The state built on Marxist–Leninist foundations has come to the end of the road.

References

Chapter 1

1. *Pravda*, 19 May 1962
2. *Khrushchev Remembers*. With an introduction, commentary and notes by Edward Crankshaw. Translated by Strobe Talbott (London 1971) p. 27

Chapter 2

1. Ibid p. 41.
2. *Rabochaya Moskva*, 9 March 1935
3. *Khrushchev Remembers* p. 45
4. *Time*, October 1, 1990 p. 73
5. N.S. Khrushchev, *Vospominaniya: Izbrannye otryvki* (New York 1979) p. 132

Chapter 3

1. *Khrushchev Remembers* p. 304
2. Frank K. Roberts 'Encounters with Khrushchev' in Martin McCauley (ed.) *Khrushchev and Khrushchevism* (London 1987) p. 217
3. Ibid p. 217
4. Y. Yevtushenko, *A Precocious Autobiography* (London

1963) p. 100
5. *Khrushchev Remembers* pp. 383–4
6. *XXII-y sezd KPSS* (Moscow 1961) Vol. 2 p. 588
7. *Vremya i my* (Tel Aviv) no. 48, 1979 pp. 164–65

Chapter 4

1. Sergei Khrushchev, *Khrushchev on Khrushchev*. Edited and translated by William Taubman (Boston MA 1990) p. 356
2. A. D. Sakharov, *O Strane i mire* (New York 1976) pp. vii–viii
3. *Time* pp. 76-7.
4. *Time* p. 77
5. *Time* p. 77
6. *Time* p. 78
7. *XXII-y sezd KPSS* (Moscow 1961) Vol 1 p. 105
8. *Time* p. 78
9. *Vremya i my* (Tel Aviv) no. 41, 1979 p. 176
10. Sergei Khrushchev, op. cit. p. 363

Chapter 5

1. Ibid p. 46
2. Ibid p. 78
3. Ibid p. 82
4. Ibid pp. 107–8
5. Ibid p. 108
6. Ibid p. 109
7. Ibid p. 136
8. Ibid p. 145
9. Ibid pp. 148–9
10. Ibid p. 150
11. Ibid p. 154
12. Ibid pp. 157–8

References

13. Ibid p. 159
14. Ibid p. 160

Chapter 6

1. Ibid p. 247
2. Ibid pp. 380–81

Select Bibliography

This section provides a brief guide to further reading on some of the topics raised in this volume. It makes no claim to be comprehensive.

There are several biographies of Khrushchev. The most comprehensive is Roy Medvedev, *Khrushchev* (Basil Blackwell, Oxford 1982). It is a more sympathetic treatment than Roy and Zhores Medvedev, *Khrushchev: The Years in Power* (Columbia University Press, New York 1977). Edward Crankshaw, *Khrushchev* (Collins, London 1966) was popular in its day and is still of interest.

Leadership politics is skilfully covered in Carl A. Linden, *Khrushchev and the Soviet Leadership* (Johns Hopkins University Press, Baltimore, MD 1966). There are several books which study Khrushchev and other Soviet leaders; eg. Seweryn Bialer, *Stalin's Successors: Leadership, Stability and Change in the Soviet Union* (Cambridge University Press, Cambridge 1980); George W. Breslauer, *Khrushchev and Brezhnev as Leaders: Building Authority as Soviet Leaders* (Allen & Unwin, London 1982); Stephen F. Cohen *et al* (eds.), *The Soviet Union since Stalin* (Macmillan, London 1980).

More wide-ranging studies are Martin McCauley (ed.), *Khrushchev and Khrushchevism* (Macmillan, London 1987) and R.F. Miller and F. Féhér (eds.), *Khrushchev and the Communist World* (Croom Helm, London 1984). Both contain some excellent essays.

On the economy see Alec Nove, *An Economic History of the USSR* (Penguin, Harmondsworth 1980). On agriculture J. F. Karcz, *The Economics of Communist Agriculture* (University of Indiana Press, Bloomington, IN 1979) is excellent. Also see Roy D. Laird (ed.), *Soviet Agricultural and Peasant Affairs* (University of Kansas Press, Kansas 1964) and W. G. Hahn, *The Politics of Soviet Agriculture 1960–70* (Johns Hopkins University Press, Baltimore, MD 1972). Martin McCauley, *Khrushchev and the Development of Soviet Agriculture: The Virgin Lands Programme 1953–64* (Macmillan, London 1976) is a detailed study of the Virgin Lands. Karl-Euguen Wädekin, *The Private Sector in Soviet Agriculture* (University of California Press, Berkeley, CA 1973) is the standard work.

On foreign policy Adam Ulam, *Expansion and Coexistence: Soviet Foreign Policy 1917–73* (Praeger, New York 1974) is still the best account of the Khrushchev era. Also excellent is Joseph L. Nogee and Robert H. Donaldson, *Soviet Foreign Policy since World War II* (Pergamon Press, New York 1981). Robert Slusser, *The Berlin Crisis of 1961* (Johns Hopkins University Press, Baltimore, MD 1973) is an exhaustive but stimulating account.

On relations with other socialist states see Z.B. Brzezinski, *The Soviet Bloc: Unity and Conflict* (Harvard University Press, Cambridge, MA 1967) which is comprehensive and stimulating; J. F. Brown, *The New Eastern Europe: the Khrushchev Era* (Praeger, New York 1966) is a good survey. Stephen Clissold (ed.), *Yugoslavia and the Soviet Union 1939–73* (Oxford University Press, London 1970) is highly recommended.

On the military Raymond L. Garthoff, *Soviet Military Policy* (Faber and Faber, London 1966) and Roman Kolkowicz, *The Soviet Military and the Communist Party* (Princeton University Press, Princeton, NJ 1967) can be recommended.

Glasnost has produced some stimulating appraisals and reminiscences about Khrushchev. Yu. V. Aksyutin (ed.), *Nikita Sergeevich Khrushchev Materialy k biografii* (Izdatelstvo politicheskoi literatury, Moscow 1989) is a valuable collection.

Khrushchev's memoirs have appeared as *Khrushchev Remembers* with an introduction, commentary and notes by Edward Crankshaw, translated by Strobe Talbott (Sphere Books, London 1971) and *Khrushchev Remembers: The Last Testament*, translated by Strobe Talbott (Deutsch, London 1974). Parts which were excised from these translations were published as *Khrushchev Remembers: The Glasnost Tapes* (Little, Brown, Boston, MA 1990). Particularly fascinating and valuable are the memoirs of Khrushchev's son Sergei Nikitich: Sergei Khrushchev, *Khrushchev on Khrushchev* edited and translated by William Taubman (Little, Brown, Boston, MA 1990).

Index

Index

Index